FLEX YOUR FEELINGS

FLEX
YOUR
FEELINGS

Train Your Brain to Develop
the 7 Traits of Emotional Fitness

Dr. Emily Anhalt

G. P. PUTNAM'S SONS
NEW YORK

PUTNAM
— EST. 1838 —

G. P. Putnam's Sons
Publishers Since 1838
An imprint of Penguin Random House LLC
1745 Broadway, New York, NY 10019
penguinrandomhouse.com

Hardcover ISBN: 9780593717615
E-book ISBN: 9780593717622
International edition ISBN: 9798217046270

Printed in the United States of America
1st Printing

Book design by Kristin del Rosario

The authorized representative in the EU for product safety and compliance is
Penguin Random House Ireland, Morrison Chambers, 32 Nassau Street,
Dublin D02 YH68, Ireland, https://eu-contact.penguin.ie.

For the feelers who are learning to think differently . . .
and the thinkers who are learning to feel more.

CONTENTS

CONTENTS

DISCLOSURE

The relationship between a therapist and their client is unique and privileged, and any information my clients disclose during their sessions is confidential and protected by a strict code of ethics and the law. The client stories in this book are either those for which I have received explicit permission from the client being described to include their anecdote, or they are anecdotes based on my clinical work as a mental health professional that have been cloaked or combined in a way to make them completely anonymized. Beyond this, any similarities or resemblances to people living or dead are purely coincidental.

The information in this book is not intended to diagnose, treat, or cure any mental health condition and is not a substitute for medical or mental health treatment. Please discuss any mental health concerns with your doctor or a licensed mental health professional. If you are experiencing a mental health crisis and are worried about your safety, don't hesitate to go to the nearest emergency room or dial 988 to reach the national Suicide & Crisis Lifeline.

FLEX YOUR FEELINGS

PART I

EMOTIONAL FITNESS IS NOT OPTIONAL

1

WHY ARE HIGH-PERFORMING PEOPLE BURNING OUT?

Just a month into 2024, beloved *Sesame Street* muppet Elmo innocently posted on the social media site X: "Elmo is just checking in! How is everyone doing?" The response to this tweet was staggering: more than 200 million likes and 20,000 responses later, the online world had spoken. "Elmo I'm gonna be real I am at my f*cking limit," one user wrote, and another confessed: "Not gonna lie . . . I'm tired, Elmo. A lot's going on, little Red." In message after message, it was evident that the massive online trauma dump touched on something that we as a society brush under the proverbial rug: we all have issues.

Emotional struggles are just part of being alive. But there is a stigma around prioritizing mental health—even as our awareness of its importance grows. Often, society frames us as either "mentally healthy" or "mentally ill"—a false dichotomy that ignores the vast majority of the population. Mental health is a spectrum that we are all on—and, in fact, most of us are in multiple places on that spectrum at any given time. We might have healthy relationships at work but not be our best selves in romantic relationships. We might feel mostly content with our lives but on some level know that we're not living out our purpose. Which means, ultimately, that we all have more work to do.

Often, we just suck it up, hoping that things will get better in time. We minimize our struggles or stuff down what we feel. If someone notices that we seem off, we deflect or say we're fine, it's really nothing. But deep down, we know it's never really nothing. To truly achieve your goals and ambitions in life—strong and supportive relationships, a thriving career or business, peak physical and mental health—you need to stand on solid emotional footing.

But if mental health is so important, why do we give it so little attention?

I'm a clinical psychologist and therapist working in Silicon Valley. I work with some of the most high-powered, hard-charging, accomplished people in the world. These are people who can identify a massive work problem, devise a strategy, and deliver results. They've worked hard to achieve their success. But it doesn't mean they're content with their lives. It doesn't mean they don't struggle.

The truth is: life is often uncomfortable, *especially* when you're aiming high. Unfortunately, our instinctive reaction to discomfort is usually to turn away. Give in to that impulse consistently, however, and you'll see a gap widen between where you are and where you want to be in life. It is usually when people realize that the gap has widened so much that they are at risk of falling down that hole that they show up in my office.

But here lies the dilemma: if you wait to work on your mental health until the wheels start falling off your emotional life—if you don't pay attention to what's going on inside your head until it really starts affecting your body—all that stress, anger, and low self-esteem will wreak havoc on your relationships, your work, and your overall satisfaction in life.

Unfortunately, many people don't realize that something needs to shift until it feels too late to change things. This way of thinking about mental health is entirely backward—it's like waiting until you're diagnosed with early signs of heart disease to start doing cardio. Instead, I encourage my clients to rethink mental health by addressing it more the way we now know we should be thinking about *physical* health: proactively. I realized that what people really need in order to keep their emotional life in shape is a proactive regimen for mental and emotional health, so that when they do hit the inevitable obstacles in life, they're able to move through them with strength, flexibility, and confidence rather than stumbling under pressure.

Can we actually train our body for mental health, just as we do for physical health? The answer is yes.

You Can't Succeed on Smarts Alone

While I was in grad school for clinical psychology, I realized that the information I was learning was being gatekept within my campus and my textbooks. At the time, there were no "emotional intelligence" classes in high school or college. People weren't flocking to social media to talk about "healthy communication" or "setting boundaries" or anyone's "growth mindset." Meditation was still fringe. And the idea of prioritizing mental health was definitely not normalized. These concepts are more mainstream today, but back then, if you weren't getting a degree in psychology, there was very little information on how to navigate relationships in a psychologically minded way. People were supposed to possess fully developed emotional coping skills, yet they were discouraged from seeking support in developing those skills or even admitting to having trouble with them. This was especially true in the context of work, as I observed firsthand with my roommate at the time, Monica.

Monica was struggling. The small-fish start-up she was working for had just been acquired by a big-fish company, and she was thrust suddenly into a massive corporate machine. From the outside, the company was well-run and highly profitable. It attracted top-tier performers, the hungry and smart, the motivated and the hardworking. The employees possessed the "right" traits typically considered important for success. In other words, they had all the hard skills to make it. But Monica would come home from work night after night to unload about what an absolute nightmare the place was, and I could tell she was overwhelmed and burned-out.

Over time and a lot of takeout, we figured out the company had made several unforced but common errors: there was ineffective communication between departments, leadership seemed to be leaking their emotional issues all over the place, and there was a severe lack of empathy for employees inside and outside of work. It all came down to overlooking or undervaluing important soft skills (a term that wildly undercuts how significant and difficult these skills are). Everyone had the business acumen and product intelligence to drive sales and profits, but not everyone had the *emotional* intelligence to make the workplace a positive and collaborative environment. And leadership didn't seem interested in doing much about it, even as attrition skyrocketed and growth sputtered. Everyone blamed the company itself, but I saw the trees through the forest: to have a healthy organization, every individual needs to feel supported to show up as a healthy version of themself.

The company was failing because the people who made it up

were struggling. Even though they were intelligent. Creative. The "best of the best." They couldn't succeed on smarts or talent alone. And neither could the business. It's true in tech, and it's true in all industries and walks of life: we bring our emotional selves to work every single day whether we like it or not. So why does our society so often privilege hard skills over interpersonal intelligence?

One big problem stemmed from the stigmas and misconceptions about emotions and mental health overall. At the time, therapy was a four-letter word, and people were discouraged from even mentioning their mental health unless they were in the throes of a crisis—and then, they were judged for having a crisis at all!

As I supported Monica in navigating her frustrations with work, I started to wonder: What if people didn't wait so long to tackle their long-suffering inner demons and seek help? Could mental health be a more proactive practice? What if we didn't wait until things were falling apart to work on our mental and emotional health? Which led me to the next question: What if we treated emotional health the way we treat physical fitness? Could we shift our mindset about mental health care to look more like going to the gym and less like going to the doctor? And what would this look like in the workplace (where we spend about a third of our lives)?

There's No Quick Fix

The importance of proactive physical fitness is both ancient and relatively new. Our ancestors had physical exercise built right into their lives, as they had to hunt for food, and, in hard times, they migrated hundreds of miles to find it. And up until the 1950s, most jobs required physical movement and labor. There was a baseline of movement in everyday life, which contributed to overall health. The downside was, of course, that a physical injury could sideline a person (and hinder their economic prospects) for good.

This baseline of movement has been slipping away as we move to an information-based society. So what have we done? We've adapted. If someone one hundred years ago had told you they were going for a run, you'd have probably wondered why—were they being chased? Jogging to improve physical health proactively is a newer idea, but it's now common sense that it's better to be proactive about your physical health instead of waiting until you're sick and then trying to fix it.

These days, many people (especially those in tech) are using their minds instead of their bodies at work. Which means, as my cofounder, Alexa Meyer, would say, *burnout* is the workplace injury of the twenty-first century. Unhealthy mind, unhealthy bottom line. At work and at home—in all aspects of our lives—it's imperative that we're as proactive with our mental and emotional health as we are with our physical health. If the world doesn't start thinking about things this way, we should brace for a global mental breakdown.

Many people like to believe that if they're not sick, they're healthy. But talk to someone who prioritizes physical fitness— someone who sleeps eight hours a night, exercises, and eats well— and they'll tell you, just because you aren't ill, does not mean you're physically fit. The same is true with emotional fitness—you might not be suffering from daily panic attacks, but that does not necessarily mean you are in good shape emotionally.

But just as a magic pill won't give you six-pack abs, there is no quick fix for work-related burnout or a troubled marriage. Transformation and personal growth demand consistent and directed effort. To develop as a human being and reach your full potential, you don't need general principles. You need a regimen. To train for a triathlon, you don't just read about running, biking, and swimming for two months. You set training goals based on your knowledge, train consistently using proven methods, and measure your progress to stay on track. You also eat well, get good sleep, and recruit emotional support from your community.

No one finishes, let alone wins, a triathlon on a whim. It takes a trusted system and a daily commitment to action. A good system says: do these things in this order, and you will achieve the expected outcome by race day. Follow the program and get the results. Why should *emotional* fitness work any differently?

The demand for help is there. Public figures are opening up about their emotional health struggles. Books, apps, and courses try to fill the gap, but no single resource has yet laid out a training regimen for emotional fitness. Experts describe emotional health without offering a path to achieving it. We spend hundreds—thousands, even—going to the gym, Pilates, and spin studios in our Lululemon outfits, but we don't spend nearly enough capital on our mental health.

I want to change that.

You Can Train for Mental Strength

My first lessons in the power of psychology were given to me by my mother. With Yoda-like wisdom, she has always had an enormous talent for synthesizing emotional turmoil into manageable and digestible lessons in human behavior.

One such moment: On a particularly trying day in middle school (weren't all days in middle school trying?), I had the experience that many young girls have of being bullied by some mean girls. That night, I sat with my mom, in tears, and asked if I should just switch schools. She told me that she could understand the desire to run away but that perhaps I had an opportunity to look inward instead.

"Emily," she said, "you have some great friends and a family that loves you, but inevitably, you're going to come across people who are less kind and have a lot of anger. Here's the thing, though—no one can hurt you with insults that you don't believe about yourself. Which means that self-compassion is the antidote to any and all hate that comes your way."

Her stunning revelations always hit exactly the way I needed them to, and they transformed my relationship with my emotions and thoughts so profoundly that they shaped my life's trajectory. I realized how powerful it could be to make space for my feelings, to examine my thoughts, to own my experiences, and to process my life as I go. I also took a psychology class in high school that taught me that when you know a lot about psychology, you know a little about everything, because the world is spoken in the language of relationships, and psychology is the study of the relationships we have to ourselves and to other people. I loved this idea—that I could learn the language of relationships—and I found myself pursuing a career in therapy so that I could support people through their struggles.

Born and raised in Silicon Valley, I developed an interest in the mindset and thought processes of entrepreneurs. During the tech boom that was happening when I was in grad school, it became clear to me that the people who are running the huge companies we all interact with are deciding a lot about our world and society, so the more mentally and emotionally healthy they are, the better off we all are. And so, when I graduated, I dove headfirst into supporting the emotional needs of business founders and other high-functioning entrepreneurs.

As you can imagine, the life of an entrepreneur demands extraordinary fortitude and flexibility. Unfortunately, most don't come to the table with the necessary emotional fitness to pull it off. As a group, these individuals tend to work even harder when the going gets tough rather than seek outside help. It's no wonder their personal problems get out of hand. Entrepreneurial meltdowns are common in the press for good reason. While the company they start may last long enough to file for an IPO, the emotionally unfit entrepreneur probably won't be there to ring the bell above the trading floor.

In my private practice, I've helped hundreds of entrepreneurs navigate these difficult waters through the development of emotional fitness. What I've come to see is that with enough sets and reps in the emotional gym of daily life, anyone can build the necessary patience, strength, character, and resilience to succeed over the long term. Working on these areas strikes many people as counterintuitive at first. These are capacities that most entrepreneurs—and most people—believe come naturally. My clinical experience proves otherwise.

As I continued to enjoy my one-on-one work with entrepreneurs, I became more and more interested in developing a proactive, large-scale approach to improving mental health for this group. To this end, I conducted clinical interviews with hundreds of psychologists and entrepreneurs about the traits of emotionally healthy leaders. A subsequent analysis of this data revealed the seven traits of emotional fitness that form the core of this book.

Findings in hand, I began consulting with some of the fastest-growing technology companies in the world, including Google,

Asana, Spotify, Salesforce, NBCUniversal, GitHub, Nasdaq, Unilever, and Bloomberg. These organizations brought me in to support their leaders in establishing emotional fitness practices to help sustain them in their work. And in 2019, I cofounded a mental health start-up, Coa, the gym for mental health. When I became a founder myself, the traits I'd been supporting others with suddenly became relevant to my own life and success in an entirely new way.

If you accept the notion that entrepreneurs run the emotional equivalent of ultramarathons, it follows that an entrepreneur's emotional training regimen should prepare *anyone* to face their own personal and professional challenges with vigor, perseverance, and often joy. Entrepreneurs are not alone in needing emotional fitness training—whether you're a doctor, teacher, parent, writer, PhD student, or CEO, training your emotional fitness will amplify and direct your efforts; buffer you against burnout, unnecessary stress, and anxiety; and cultivate an inner sense of satisfaction and fulfillment.

And, most important, it will improve your relationships. As psychotherapist and relationship expert Esther Perel says, "The quality of your relationships determines the quality of your life," and the relationship you have with yourself is the place to start. What you hold in your hands is a manual to better emotional health—a comprehensive, research-backed program for developing all the key traits of emotional fitness to face any and all of life's challenges. It offers a way to think and feel differently and, thus, show up in your life differently.

You don't have to be broken.

You don't have to be in crisis.

You don't have to be anything but ready to level up and move closer toward the version of yourself that you want to be.

Ready? Let's get into it.

2
WHAT DOES AN EMOTIONALLY FIT PERSON LOOK LIKE?

*If you need to pass some eye water, I'll be happy to
go out and get you some weakness tissues.*

—JACK WELCH, FORMER CHAIRMAN AND CEO OF
GENERAL ELECTRIC, PLAYING HIMSELF ON *30 ROCK*

David was a thirty-seven-year-old consultant at a hot San Francisco–based AI tech company, but that was just his day job—his real passion was ultramarathon running. He had run dozens of races around the world in some of the most inhospitable terrains, from the Ultra Trail du Mont Blanc in France to the Marathon des Sables in Morocco. Not only did he finish these marathons battling extreme conditions like desert heat and torrential rain, but he also beat out world-class competitors. When it came to running, he was on top of his game.

Where he wasn't on top of his game was at his job, and he had come to me because he had been put on a performance-improvement plan. While his work output was quite strong, his boss flagged him for having too many interpersonal issues. He was seen as argumentative, unempathetic, and uncollaborative by the rest of his team. He had, according to his review, "no people skills." His hard skills—doubling the company's number of clients in record time—had gotten him noticed by the higher-ups, but unfortunately, his lack of "soft skills" was stopping him from achieving more.

David had a sense that his peers didn't like him, but he wasn't sure how to change this, or—when he first stepped into my office—if he even *wanted* to. In his mind, he was just doing his job; he held himself to a high standard and expected everyone else to perform at his level. If his colleagues didn't like it, that was on them. When team members tried to explain to him that his communication style felt dismissive and unkind, he waved them off. Ten minutes into our first session, I'd already gotten a taste of it.

"How are you feeling about starting this work with me?" I asked.

"Ah, so I guess we're already getting into the 'let's talk about your feelings' bullshit, huh?"

"Well, David, admittedly I don't think talking about feelings is bullshit, but you *are* giving me some sense of why your colleagues find you combative." I gave him a sly smile.

David winced and then laughed.

"Sorry. I know. I'm not thrilled about how things are going there, either. I'm just not so sure there's anything I can do about it. I think this is just who I am."

"You know, in my experience, anyone who says 'this is just who I am' about something that's holding them back has never experienced really good therapy. 'Who you are' is an ever-evolving truth, and together we can shift the things that aren't working."

David was skeptical.

"Let me ask you something, David. How did you go from being a good runner to being an extraordinary runner?"

"I trained. I trained every single day."

"That makes sense. And you probably had some quality coaches and community along the way, right?"

"Definitely."

"All right, then. So you have some sense of what it takes to get fit. And that's what we're going to do here, together. We're going to help you train your emotional fitness."

David was open to giving it a try, and from there, we got down to work. Every week, David and I met and talked about his life. Over time, he really opened up—he talked about his feelings, his thoughts, his past relationships, and his hopes for the future. He came up with emotional goals he wanted to achieve, and we talked about what it would take to get there and what might have kept him from getting there already. We took baby steps toward healthier relationships. He practiced communicating his needs more empathetically, learned how to create some space between his anger and his actions, leaned into being more playful and collaborative, and took ownership over the role he was playing in his own life. David's relationships at work (and at home) began to improve. And he noticed himself enjoying his job a lot more as a result. David was doing the work, and he was enjoying the fruits of his labor.

In short, he was becoming more emotionally fit.

A New Emotional Landscape at Work

In my twenty years of studying and practicing psychology, I have helped hundreds of Silicon Valley highfliers improve their emotional health. But it wasn't so long ago that the phrase *emotional health* was barely uttered in the workplace. For too long, basic management skills didn't leave much room for emotional display. Success was ruled by numbers, not by people, and killer negotiating chops won the day—any day—over emoting effectively. Hard skills were prioritized over soft skills.

Cracks in the "if you want to cry, do it outside" exterior began to show in the early 2000s, driven in part by the concept of emotional intelligence (the ability to identify and manage one's own emotions, as well as the emotions of others), which fostered engagement and better communication in the workplace. Since then, self-help and management books, corporate off-site retreats, and HR seminars on communication (Zoom breakout room, anyone?) have attempted to raise awareness about the importance of a well-balanced inner life.

But perhaps the biggest fault line was created by something we haven't ever seen before: the confluence of several different generations in the workplace. Baby boomers and Gen Xers, who were raised to have steely exteriors, are rubbing elbows with millennials and Gen Zers, who want (and rightfully demand) a more thoughtful approach that ensures a better and more fulfilling work-life balance. Four different generations—all with very different philosophies on emotions and success, and all trying to get along but not quite sure how to do it.

It doesn't help that society continues to downplay the role of emotional well-being. Why? For one, our educational system fails to help young people prepare for the mental and emotional stressors of modern life, from social media that promotes bad behavior and impossible lifestyle standards to political ideologies that have fractured communities, to the existential threat of climate change and unrelenting gun violence. And for all the media coverage, celebrity confessions, and the propagation of virtual-therapy apps, there remains an enormous stigma around mental health struggles. Even now, it feels taboo to ask for help dealing with emotions, above all at work. When it comes to how you feel inside, you're pretty much on your own out there.

That's where I come in.

My clients run the gamut: I have old-school types who believe that feelings are best left at home (as though that's humanly possible). I have perfectionists, shaken, not stirred with a splash of narcissism (because in the tech world, you have to believe in something no one else sees yet). And I have bleeding-heart young go-getters who aren't sure how to manage their emotions in a workplace setting. I also see those who have to work *with* these personalities and feel they need to match that same intensity or that they have to prove themselves, only to end up feeling overworked, undervalued, or left out of the proverbial boys' club altogether.

Why Do People Struggle with Emotions?

There are a variety of reasons a person might not thrive emotionally. Some are controllable and some aren't, but paying attention to your emotional state is crucial because it affects your relationships with family, friends, and work colleagues. As with many things, knowledge is power—and knowing what may be causing your distress is the first step to feeling better (we'll get into this more in chapter 5).

THE COMPANY YOU KEEP

Emotional health leads to healthy relationships, and healthy relationships lead to good emotional health. Caring, supportive relationships are a key factor for your emotional health and satisfy your need for connection, while unhealthy, toxic relationships will keep a harmful cycle going. Your earliest relationships were the blueprint you've built your life on and have shaped you, for better or worse (if you think the way you relate to your boss has nothing to do with the way you related to your parents growing up, think again). When you were young, you had minimal choices and tools at your disposal. You didn't get to choose where you lived, where you went to school, or who your family members were. So you did the best you could with the limited set of tools and resources you did have. Often that meant building emotional walls and avoiding things that felt unsafe. The skill of coping with life's demands is learned like any other. Some people were lucky enough to have been taught the basics in a stable and nurturing home growing up. Others, not so much. In any case, your early experiences and relationships affect you to this day—both positively and negatively—and play a role in your overall emotional health and how you relate to others.

GENES

Some people may have a genetic predisposition to certain mental health conditions, which can affect their well-being. When it comes to the greatly debated question of nature versus nurture, I believe both influence us to various degrees, depending on the individual and their circumstances. But in general, I tend to believe that nature loads the gun and nurture pulls the trigger, meaning that our predispositions are affected by certain environments or situations. But all conditions, when properly understood, can be managed, mitigated, and, often, changed and healed.

STRESS MESS

Major life events, such as the death of a loved one, divorce, job loss, or any kind of trauma can cause significant stress, which in turn can affect your emotional health. Even small losses or changes in life, when ignored, can dramatically affect how you show up emotionally day-to-day. Feelings of burnout, impostor syndrome, anxiety, depression, and emotional distress have hit an all-time high, but I'm hard-pressed to find statistics that accurately reflect this collective malaise. McKinsey Health Institute's 2022 survey found that, on average, one in four employees have experienced symptoms of burnout, and this is global, not just in the United States. And in 2020, the National Center for Health Statistics reported that 40 percent of Americans suffered from symptoms of anxiety and depression. I believe both stats are woefully underrepresentative, and the pandemic didn't help: in addition to global uncertainty, job loss, health struggles, and living in survival mode for three years, a newly hybrid work environment is blurring the line between our work and home lives. All this can lead to more stress and burnout.

PHYSICAL HEALTH

It has been widely shown that there is a strong correlation between physical and emotional health. The mind-body connection is real, and those who ignore it are doing themselves a huge disservice. Dr. Bessel van der Kolk and his book, *The Body Keeps the Score*, broke ground with his theories on the interplay between the body and mind when it comes to trauma. It's a two-way street: as much as emotional ills can negatively affect your physical body, chronic physical illnesses or pain can negatively affect your emotional health. Similarly, an unhealthy lifestyle (poor diet, lack of exercise, substance abuse, and insufficient sleep) can wreak havoc on your emotions.

CULTURAL AND SOCIETAL EXPECTATIONS

A positive self-image and healthy self-esteem are important components of emotional health, but both have taken a nosedive in the advent of social media, where comparing your behind-the-scenes world to everyone else's online highlight reel has increased hundred-fold. Sociological factors such as systemic racism and wealth inequality, as well as long-held stigmas around socioeconomic status, neurodivergence, and the LGBTQ+ community are still present and deeply problematic. A persistently skewed health care system is a huge part of the problem, and across the board, fewer marginalized people seek treatment because of a myriad of reasons such as cost, access, and stigma. For example, 25 percent of African Americans seek mental health services when they need them, compared to 40 percent of white Americans. When it comes to emotional health, we're stuck in a catch-22—we need healthy individuals if we are to create a healthier society, but an unhealthy society makes it very difficult to be a healthy individual. As psychologist and author Viktor Frankl says, "An abnormal reaction to an abnormal situation is normal behavior." There is *a lot* of work to be done here, we have a very long way to go.

While these factors can affect each person differently depending on life circumstances, everyone grapples with the same taboo when it comes to talking about mental and emotional health. It's important to fight the stigma and make it more permissible to tend to these issues *before* a person starts fraying at the seams. Otherwise, hidden emotional struggles can sabotage physical health and happiness. Unfortunately, for every person who rages under stress, there are ten more who suffer silently: frozen by self-doubt, incapacitated by anxiety, or just generally unsatisfied with life. It's time to change that.

What Does an Emotionally Healthy Person Look Like?

As I developed my idea about reframing mental health to be more like physical fitness, I began using the term *emotional fitness*—I noticed this term resonated with people who felt themselves to be mostly healthy but still wanted to level up their mental health—and I decided to do some research about what an emotionally fit person looks like in real life. I knew that similar to physical fitness, emotional fitness would not just be an absence of disorders. Being emotionally fit would include being able to create and maintain meaningful and rewarding relationships with family, friends, romantic partners, colleagues, and oneself, as well as a sense of satisfaction about life in general and where it was headed.

But, I wondered, what tools does a person need to get there? What attributes make it possible to live an emotionally fit life? To answer these questions, I conducted a comprehensive research study called an interpretive phenomenological analysis—a fancy way of saying that I interviewed one hundred psychologists and entrepreneurs and asked a series of questions to figure out what an emotionally healthy person looked and felt like to them. I wanted to be able to put a name to the qualities that measured emotional health. I asked the therapists a series of questions, such as: When you are in a session with someone, how do you know that they're emotionally healthy? What does it look like when a person goes from being less emotionally healthy to more emotionally healthy? What changes do you see? How do you measure your own emotional health? With the entrepreneurs, I asked a different set of questions, such as: What makes you feel like you are engaging in an emotionally healthy way with people at work? What does an emotionally healthy leader look like and feel like? What is it about certain colleagues that makes them more enjoyable to work with? How about those colleagues you don't like working with?

Over the course of a year or so, I collected the data. As I pored over the answers and coded the interviews for themes and patterns, key concepts emerged: I recognized, like a fuzzy picture coming into focus, the seven traits that emotionally healthy people have in common. I called them the **Seven Traits of Emotional Fitness**. Here's how those seven traits unfolded.

1. Many therapists I interviewed cited the importance of tolerating discomfort. Emotionally healthy clients, they told me, could sit with some uncertainty, because growth is nearly impossible if a person does not have some ability to be uncomfortable. Entrepreneurs echoed this trait. Starting a company from scratch is close to futile, and along the way, rejection and uncertainty are inevitable, so the ability to withstand the ups and downs of life and business are necessary for success. This simple (and yet profoundly difficult) practice of becoming more comfortable being uncomfortable is **MINDFULNESS**. I made this the first trait because developing the rest of the traits requires an ability to withstand some discomfort.

2. Both camps flagged defensiveness as a hindrance to emotional health. For their part, therapists commented that their clients often come to see them not because *they want to change* but because they're hoping the therapist will tell them *how to change everyone around them*. They want to keep their defenses up and do exactly what they're doing but feel better about it. But a sign of emotional health peeks through when a person starts to realize, "Oh, *I* have to change. I need to be willing to take responsibility for how I show up if I want things to change around me." The entrepreneurs appreciated those who asked a lot of questions and genuinely wanted to know what they could do to be better at their job and support people more effectively. It was taking responsibility for themselves that scored high marks. This act of pursuing growth

over defensiveness is **CURIOSITY**. Everyone is defensive sometimes, but to prioritize growth over comfort, one must learn to get curious and ask questions.

3. It's hard to change something before you know it exists, but humans work so hard *not* to know things about themselves. Many therapists I interviewed mentioned that they'd know progress was being made when clients began acknowledging their frustrations and becoming more open to seeing parts of themselves they had previously avoided. Entrepreneurs, for their part, painted disparate pictures of how the worst leaders were completely unaware of the effect they had on the people around them. But the healthy leaders among them, on the other hand, were able to own what they brought to the table. This is **SELF-AWARENESS**: the ability to understand your personality traits, triggers, biases, strengths, struggles, tendencies, and characteristics that make up, well, you.

4. Words like *grit* and *perseverance* came up a lot in my research. Therapists saw emotionally healthy people as being able to push forward through setbacks and failures but not do so mindlessly. Their healthy clients were the ones who could experience a difficult thing, honor the experience in a way that fostered learning (versus just surviving), and grow as a result. The entrepreneurs talked about the importance of a leader being able to stay the course and not give up, no matter how many times they were knocked down. They mentioned the ability to handle failures and not crumble under the weight of them. This is **RESILIENCE**, and it is the ability to bounce forward, grow, and learn from your setbacks, disappointments, failures, and difficult experiences.

5. To be emotionally healthy and have quality relationships, therapists and entrepreneurs alike agreed on the importance of a caring mindset and an ability to put oneself in other people's shoes regularly. Therapists mentioned that their emotionally healthy clients were willing and able to allow themselves to feel what other people around them were feeling. Both the therapists and the entrepreneurs saw the need for confidently navigating an environment where emotions are at play, whether at home or work. The ability to meet people where they are and truly understand and care about other people's emotions is critical for human connection. This is **EMPATHY**.

6. Both groups underscored the importance of effectively sharing ideas and thoughts with others. The therapists described their emotionally healthy clients as people who could identify what they're feeling and what they need, and communicate those feelings and needs effectively (rather than expecting people to read their minds). The entrepreneurs described the importance of being able to deliver clear expectations and set goals, all while being a great motivator. They also spoke about giving—and receiving!—feedback well. What they were all describing is good **COMMUNICATION**. Putting words to your needs and expectations is vital for emotional health.

7. The final trait surprised me until I realized how obvious it is. Therapists described someone as emotionally healthy if they could entertain an idea without feeling too attached to it. Their healthy clients were not rigid, their thinking wasn't so black-or-white, and they could ponder different outcomes. Entrepreneurs saw emotional health in people who could brainstorm, collaborate, and offer lots of room to be creative. It may not be obvious at first, but both camps are saying the

same thing: it's important to be able to play. **PLAYFULNESS** might not be a word that comes up in people's minds when they think about emotional health, but ultimately, a lot of therapy is just teaching people how to play—to remove constraints and think big. The ability to "play well with others" is a lesson we're supposed to learn in kindergarten, but it can be a struggle for plenty of adults.

After sketching out these seven traits, I needed to see if they would stand the test of time and real-life conditions. Over the years, I championed them in front of hundreds of companies and conferences. I collected real-time feedback from people all over the world, and with my one-on-one clients, I sought to pinpoint which traits needed the most support and developed a plan to help them train. Over time, I concluded that, indeed, these seven traits hold up. Much like physical fitness, which includes concepts of aerobic endurance, strength, and flexibility, these seven traits serve as the foundation of what it means to be healthy emotionally. And just as a fitness regimen works out different parts of the body and requires a good diet and sleep habits to improve overall physical health, each of these traits builds off the others to improve overall emotional health.

These seven emotional traits work in tandem to make you stronger as a whole: as you increase your ability to withstand discomfort (mindfulness), you'll be better able to lower your defenses (curiosity) and learn about yourself (self-awareness). This knowledge will equip you to get through difficult moments in life (resilience), which will set you up to support (empathy) and connect with (communication) others. Meeting people in this way will make it possible to think big and be creative (playfulness), which will create an environment in which you'll continue to strengthen every other trait.

What Emotional Fitness Is *Not*

There is a lot of noise out there, in real life and online, about what emotional health looks like. Some of it is good, but I'm going to level with you: a lot of it is pop-psychology bullshit. As with any good fitness program, let's start by sorting the signals from the noise. Here are a few things that emotional fitness is *not*:

EMOTIONAL FITNESS IS NOT A QUICK FIX.

Americans are all about the quick fix, but just as you can't do one push-up or eat a stalk of broccoli and call it a day with physical fitness, you're going to have to play the long game for good emotional fitness. You might wish that getting a handle on your emotions could be as easy as getting food delivered through an app, but you need to get out of the mindset that everything should have been fixed yesterday. Your emotional life is complicated, and you should stop trying to find easy solutions for complicated problems. It takes practice, and it takes work, but believe me, it *does* work. As adults, we sometimes forget that if we practice something we aren't good at, we *will* get better at it—it just takes time and dedication. And as you do this work on yourself, things will change around you. As you get healthier, healthier people will just start to show up in your life.

EMOTIONAL FITNESS IS NOT "SELF-CARE."

Most people see working on themselves as a frivolous practice—a nice-to-have, not a must-have. Self-care is a vague and slightly woo-woo term reserved for people with privilege and too much time on their hands. Working people must, well . . . work, to get what they want. No one who attempts the emotional workouts that follow would dismiss them as frivolous. This practice is so much more than taking a spa day, a staycation to binge Netflix, or a silent retreat to find yourself. It's important to take time off, of course, but emotional fitness takes work and practice; it certainly won't be attained by a mere afternoon of drinking Aperol spritzes. These workouts are tough as hell and offer dramatic, real-world benefits. Instead of "self-care," think "self-maintenance."

EMOTIONAL FITNESS IS NOT TOXIC POSITIVITY.

Have you ever shared a challenging situation with someone and had them tell you that it's "for the best"? That you should "keep your head up" or "smile through it"? Beware of *toxic positivity*. This newish term refers to the belief you should always look on the bright side and remain positive—no matter the circumstance—while stifling more negative emotions. Phrases like "everything happens for a reason" or "there's always a silver lining" ignore the other half of the truth—that life includes some suffering. It always will. It's important not to pathologize or shove down normal, human pain. Emotional fitness validates the full range of human emotions, all of which have a place in your life. And speaking of the full range of emotions . . .

EMOTIONAL FITNESS IS NOT CONSTANT HAPPINESS.

Emotional fitness is a sustainable state of well-being—being able to effectively manage stress and emotions and relate well to others. We live in a culture that fetishizes happiness—we're made to feel like something is wrong with us if we're not thrilled about every moment. But happiness is an elevated state, and is not unwaveringly sustainable. It is only one of many healthy, useful, important emotions that will help you be emotionally strong. Rather than focusing on simply being happier, think about how to increase the depth and authenticity of your satisfaction with your life. It is all about gaining and recognizing the *agency* you have in your own life. Agency is the power you have over your life and choices. It's about your ability to take action in difficult situations and take responsibility for your decisions, and your capacity to influence your own thoughts and behavior so you can live your life the way you want to instead of feeling like life is happening *to* you.

EMOTIONAL FITNESS IS NOT REACTIVE.

It's proactive. No sensible person would ignore a grinding noise coming from their car engine. Yet we exhort each other to "rise and grind" and push ourselves beyond our limits. If you perform regular maintenance on your car, you should invest at least as much effort in tuning up your mental health. Celebrate the hustle all you want, but don't skip the requisite tire rotations and oil changes. The average F1 driver makes several pit stops in a single race. That means instead of running yourself ragged every day, between work, social life, family duties—give yourself pit stops to recharge and work on your emotional health *before* it becomes a huge struggle. I understand the desire to work hard and push through exhaustion, fear, or sadness—it is a common message to receive: suck it up. But that much grinding and spinning your wheels will only ruin your engine.

How This Book Works

I'm not going to sugarcoat it, emotional fitness requires work and commitment, just like physical fitness does. But I promise that the work will pay off. This program will energize and motivate you to flex your feels and break an emotional sweat. It will help you understand and appreciate all the core concepts you'll need to become emotionally fit, and even at the start you will notice improvements in the texture of your everyday life. Each of the following chapters will be devoted to one of the seven traits, taking a deep look at how it contributes to your overall emotional health and how you can actionably "flex" that trait in your life.

If you do your reps and hone these traits to their fullest, you will see real-time results: you will learn from criticism instead of collapsing under it, you will build and maintain healthier relationships, you will increase your ability to resolve interpersonal conflicts, and you will be better able to achieve your deeply held ambitions. Not overnight, of course. It takes time and practice. Keeping active requires consistent effort, and there are many different levels of fitness, from someone who is just starting to run, to doing their first 5K, to becoming an elite marathoner who has been running for decades. Whatever level you're starting from, keep going—you will progress. Small steps lead to big change.

My favorite metaphor to use for emotional fitness is of a ship changing course. A large ship or carrier can't turn on a dime. It's a slow process and is barely, if at all, perceptible in the moment. If a ship changes its direction by only one degree, no one on board (or watching from shore) will notice. But look at where that ship is an hour, a week, or a month later, and you'll see that one degree of change translates to a completely different position in the sea. When it comes to your emotional fitness, it won't always feel like things are changing in the moment, but if you work on it consistently, you can trust that your life will be subtly directed toward profound change over time.

Testing, Testing

Speaking of change, you'll want to actively track your emotional fitness progress along the way. To help you gauge where you are now, take this simple quiz. On a scale of 1 to 5 (with 1 meaning *This is a huge struggle for me* and 5 meaning *This is a huge strength for me*), how emotionally fit do you feel in each of the seven traits? Let's take each trait one by one.

MINDFULNESS: Do you lean into and embrace your discomfort rather than avoiding it? A mindful person is willing to be uncomfortable in order to grow.

1   2   3   4   5

CURIOSITY: Do you have a learning mindset? Can you take in tough feedback and ask tough questions? A curious person actively seeks to learn more about themself and others.

1   2   3   4   5

SELF-AWARENESS: Do you have a strong sense of self and know your triggers, biases, and emotions? A self-aware person recognizes their strengths and shortcomings.

1   2   3   4   5

RESILIENCE: Do you face life's challenges head-on and use them as an opportunity to learn and grow? A resilient person doesn't let setbacks, well, set them back (for too long).

1   2   3   4   5

EMPATHY: Do you let yourself feel the emotions and see the perspectives of others? An empathetic person can and does regularly put themself in others' shoes.

1   2   3   4   5

COMMUNICATION: Do you clearly express your needs and expectations, and listen to others in kind? A communicative person can effectively exchange ideas and thoughts.

1   2   3   4   5

PLAYFULNESS: Do you approach life with a "yes, and . . ." mindset and foster a safe space for connection and creativity? A playful person can think big and exist "in the gray."

1   2   3   4   5

Where Do We Go from Here?

To increase these numbers, you'll need to get your reps in. Just as every fitness regimen includes exercises (e.g., physical push-ups) to help you get stronger, each chapter in this book includes trait-specific exercises, or what I like to call "emotional push-ups." Emotional push-ups are small emotional exertions that put you just a little outside of your comfort zone so you can grow. Like real push-ups, the more you do them, the easier they get and the more you can do. They'll help you get emotionally stronger now and prepare you for times of stress and uncertainty later.

An emotional push-up could be anything from apologizing for a mistake to asking for feedback from a direct report to letting yourself cry at a sad movie. Remember as you read on, what's just outside of one person's comfort zone might be way outside of another's. While I will provide general prompts for the push-ups, how you practice them will be dependent on the particular emotional "muscle" you want to flex and where you are in your emotional fitness journey. For example, if you're a person who says yes to everything that's asked of you only to end up feeling overwhelmed and resentful, an emotional push-up for you might be giving a (firm but kind) "no" to one request today. But if you're a person who tends to put your own needs above others, a push-up might look like helping someone else with a task.

As the philosopher and Roman emperor Marcus Aurelius wrote, "The soul becomes dyed with the color of its thoughts." If you change your thoughts, you can change your whole world. I do believe that there's something very powerful about thinking about things in a new way. But you can't think your way out of a feeling; rather, you have to feel your way *through* that feeling. Both your mind and your emotional state are important tools for emotional fitness.

Leaning into your feelings is the first step you'll take on the road to emotional fitness, and that means you are going to get a bit uncomfortable. You need to get comfortable with discomfort, because you're going to experience plenty of it in this book. Instead of ignoring or turning away from your discomfort, you need to show up and look at it in the eyes. Think of this trait as tying up your shoelaces and getting in some active stretches before you head off on your run. You need to get mentally ready to do the work. So put on your running shoes, and let's talk about our first trait: **mindfulness**.

PART II

THE BUILDING BLOCKS OF EMOTIONAL FITNESS

3

MINDFULNESS
Getting Uncomfortable

Oh sure, I love going with the flow; I just need to
know when the flow starts. And where it's going.
And what time it'll get there.

—A POPULAR TIKTOK VOICEOVER

Meghan—a young and talented go-getter in sales at a large branding agency—heard the familiar *ding* of an incoming email as she sat down at her desk one Tuesday morning. It was from her boss, Talia. *That's weird,* she thought, *I don't typically hear from her until the end of the day for a check-in.* Coffee in one hand, mouse in the other, Meghan clicked open the email. It read: "Can we get on a video call in an hour?" No niceties, no elaboration, no sign-off.

Odd, Meghan thought. Something was up, and Meghan did not want to wait an hour to find out what it was.

"Of course! Can you tell me what the call will be about?" Meghan responded.

Talia didn't reply.

Meghan emailed one more time. "Any info you can share would be great, thanks!"

Still, nothing. Meghan tried to focus on her work, but the knot in her stomach had other plans. Finally, an hour later, Meghan logged in. After their hellos, Talia got to the heart of her call.

"I wanted to bring up something that happened on your sales call yesterday. You were super prepared, as usual, and I see you having a great future here. But something happened that I need to address. If this were the first time, I would have let it go, but I've noticed a pattern on several occasions."

Talia continued: "At the end of the call, when the customer insisted that he'd need some time to confer with his team, you cut him off and demanded to know when you'd have an answer. I know that sales is all about persistence, but I've noticed that you seem to have a lot of trouble waiting and giving people the time they need to make decisions. I love your can-do attitude and that you don't take no for an answer, but I need you to be more patient. Just today I saw it happen with my email—you demanded twice to know what this call would be about even though we would be talking in just an hour."

Meghan got the message. She was never good at waiting, and she knew she could be demanding. But isn't pushing for a yes a *good* thing for a salesperson? Shouldn't Talia have been praising her for her persistence and drive? Weren't these the very traits that had led to her success in the first place?

Meghan was puzzled by Talia's feedback, but she could see that *something* wasn't working, so she came to see me. In our first session, Meghan cut to the chase and relayed her frustrations at work. She wanted to be a team player, but she also wanted to know why her wings had been clipped. Could I help her figure it out? And if so, how long would it take, and what did she need to do to get there? Was therapy going to take a week, a month, a year? She wanted to know the play-by-play.

It didn't take long to appreciate what her boss might have been trying to point out to her.

I responded the way I always do when people are anxious to know all the answers yesterday: "I'm happy to share a bit about what to expect, but the way this process works is that sometimes we won't know where we need to go until we're on our way there. But we're going to find our way together, and we can check in along the way. Okay?"

Unfortunately, this seemed to distress her more than comfort her. And after a few more sessions, her pattern was clear: She couldn't bear uncertainty. She hated not knowing the next move. She didn't let things unfold naturally. She was a type A personality who bristled at the words *I don't know*. Meghan was obsessed with schedules, routines, and knowing everything there is to know so she could dot the *i*'s and cross the *t*'s. This was a strength in many ways—she was organized, hardworking, and rarely missed important details in her job. But it was getting in the way of her relationships at work and at home.

Meghan told me that nothing drove her crazier than when her friends wanted to "play things by ear" on a Saturday night. She would insist that a plan be made in advance, which seemed to put everyone off. "But if I don't make the plans, we waste so much time just hanging around," she explained, unable to grasp that this downtime was, to her friends, a feature not a bug. Meghan was noticing that she was being invited to fewer and fewer events. While she was clearly the most dependable in her group of friends, she was also flagged as the one who couldn't be flexible or spontaneous. Read: no fun.

I felt this lack of spontaneity in my sessions with Meghan as well, and I saw this in her behavior in a number of ways. One of those ways was her inability to sit in silence. Every time our conversation paused, even for a moment, Meghan jumped to fill the void. I noticed this early on but let it go at first.

Eventually, I decided to mention it. "I wonder if you feel uncomfortable sitting quietly with your thoughts and feelings here."

"You know," she confessed nervously, "it's not only uncomfortable here, it's uncomfortable for me everywhere. I *hate* awkward silences. So much so that if there's a brief pause in conversation, I put my foot in my mouth and say something unnecessary or cut someone off who was about to talk. I know I should be making space for other people, but moments of quiet make me cringe. I hate waiting to see what will happen. I'd rather just control it myself. And maybe that's why I can be so demanding on my sales calls—I either want to land the deal or know right away that it isn't going to happen."

Now we were getting somewhere.

To keep the momentum, I asked about Meghan's past. "Has this always felt true for you—the need to fill the space or know what's going to happen next? Has going with the flow always been tough?"

"Yes." Meghan described her childhood as fairly chaotic, with parents who fought a lot. Anger was the emotion of the day, and silences were usually the calm right before a storm. Going with the flow never felt like an option because the flow was always scary. It only meant more chaos.

"I had to make sure things happened in a way that would keep the peace. If I didn't, things got very upsetting very quickly."

Meghan's eyes flickered with the realization of what she had just said. I could see her make the connection from her childhood to twenty years later, where any uncertainty sparked that same eerie feeling that something bad was about to happen. Her long-standing perception of foreboding had stopped her from enjoying those in-between moments, but her attempt to avoid the discomfort by making a plan or filling the space led to feelings of shame and embarrassment—a complicated trade-off.

Meghan's story is just one example of how people avoid feeling uncomfortable, and it doesn't necessarily have to originate from a difficult childhood experience like hers. It's human nature to want to stay with what feels familiar, safe, and anxiety-free. We are creatures of habit, the adage goes, and our brains are hardwired to resist change. Important shifts such as leaving a relationship that isn't working, starting a new job, or having a tough conversation can all stir up discomfort since they're full of difficult moments and unknowable outcomes. Will I be happy? Will I be good at my job? Will I know what to say? Instead of letting go, you hold on for fear of failing or making a mistake, and you may make decisions based on that fear: you stay in the unhealthy relationship, reject the job offer, or avoid the conversation. You become rigid in your ways. You turn to coping mechanisms that maintain a certain status quo and may provide a false state of comfort—but little growth.

I can relate to all this: I, too, used to have trouble with silence, especially when I first started as a therapist. In my freshman naivete, I couldn't wait to jump in and say something helpful or ask a question. I was eager to put everything I learned into practice, but what I *hadn't* learned in school was simple and so important: to sit quietly and allow space for clients to contemplate what had been said in the room. My work became much more powerful once I learned silence was a catalyst for reflection and growth. So when Meghan shared her discomfort with me, not only was I able to empathize with her, I could show her the amazing world that opened up in silence and uncertainty.

And we did indeed open up an amazing world. After talking about her past, we brought things back into the present. We dissected that sales call where she had cut off her potential customer. I asked her how she had felt after she spoke out of turn.

"There's a push-pull of feelings: To do my job well, I need to be persistent. But on the other hand, I can tell people don't like being strong-armed into making decisions. Waiting is just so uncomfortable, though. What if the customer came back to me a day later and said no? I would rather just know that right away. But it's super embarrassing to think that my impatience is annoying people."

So here is the quandary Meghan made for herself: the discomfort she was trying to avoid (uncertainty) created a more problematic and discomforting situation (turmoil at work and at home). The ironic truth is, the things you do to avoid discomfort often end up being *more* uncomfortable and worse for you than the original thing you were trying to avoid, as it was for Meghan.

This can manifest itself in many situations. Imagine you're tired and overwhelmed at work and a colleague asks you to help with a task. If you're a person who feels uncomfortable saying no and asserting your boundaries, you might agree to take on the task to avoid a difficult conversation. Suddenly, you're drowning in all the work you have to do and resent the colleague who asked for help, even though they had no idea you were already overworked. Now, you're in multiple uncomfortable situations because you couldn't tolerate the discomfort of saying no.

Ostriches don't actually stick their heads in the sand to hide from predators, but the myth persists as a metaphor because people do it all the time. Do you reach for your phone at night because you can't put your thoughts to bed and need to distract yourself? Do you sidestep conflict with a friend even when their behavior bothers you? Do you stay with a less-than-ideal partner to avoid being alone? A good friend of mine found herself in a toxic relationship in her thirties. She was desperately unhappy, but ending it would mean a lot of discomfort—breaking a lease, buying new furniture, making new friends—she worried it would be too uncomfortable to start over. So rather than face reality and move forward, she kept her head buried in the sand for two more years. There's no getting that time back now.

An Uncomfortable Truth

No one *likes* discomfort, but I can promise you this: every single thing you want in your work and personal life lives on the other side of discomfort.

No one who has ever achieved anything spectacular did so without withstanding some discomfort. The ability to tolerate the tough parts of life—difficult emotions, uncomfortable realities, challenging situations—and not run away toward comfort too quickly is called mindfulness. It's a muscle you can (and must) develop to show up strong and healthy in your career and in your life.

So, what does someone who employs a strong muscle of mindfulness look like? They make the best decision at any given moment instead of the one that's most comfortable. They think their uncomfortable thoughts and feel their uncomfortable feelings. They do what they need to do even when it's tough. They pursue growth instead of stagnation. In short—they are comfortable being uncomfortable. Whether you hope to run a business, run a marathon, or run for office, you need to be able to mindfully sit with unpleasant thoughts and feelings without stuffing them down, avoiding them, or numbing them.

Mindfulness is the first trait of emotional fitness because all the following traits in this book will depend on you flexing this emotional muscle. In other words, to be emotionally fit, you'll need to be willing to get a bit uncomfortable. Just like with any physical fitness program, if you can't endure a bit of discomfort, you aren't going to improve. Lifting only a comfortable amount of weight? Running only a comfortable distance? You probably aren't getting any stronger or fitter. Why do you think Nike's "Just Do It" ad campaign is so popular that the company still uses the motto across all their branding initiatives, nearly forty years after its conception? It's a simple and direct prompt that we can't always wait for something to feel easy to get started.

And that goes for your emotional health as well as your physical health. Staying emotionally comfortable is tempting, but doing the same thing day in and day out dulls your senses. You'll become complacent, tuned out, dialed down. You probably won't accomplish or even try many new things. It's the opposite of growth. Avoiding discomfort in the short term leads to stagnation—or, worse, regression—in the long term. Discomfort, on the other hand, opens options and possibilities. It allows for growth, learning, and excitement. When you make that leap and keep at it, what was once seemingly impossible will become doable. Of course, the goal is not to push yourself past discomfort and into panic or pain. It's to explore your discomfort and lean into it just enough to grow. Master the practice of mindfully sitting in discomfort, and you'll get places you never thought possible.

So if tolerating discomfort helps increase learning, success, and, of course, emotional fitness, why do people fight it with every fiber of their being? And why do we all have so much trouble sitting with uncomfortable emotions when they do arise?

First, and tragically: many people are not given the support, permission, and tools in their childhood to feel their more difficult or complex emotions, so they learn to turn away from that discomfort wherever they can, much like Meghan. They often don't even realize they're doing it. They learn to hide their feelings with well-worn coping mechanisms that can often become more problematic than the actual feelings they're burying. They may drink too much, overeat, overspend, or engage in any other activity that distracts them when they're feeling down. The tricky truth is, they're not outsmarting discomfort here—they're just avoiding and compounding it.

In my experience, it is not your emotions but your *resistance* to your emotions that will hurt you. To achieve your ambitions as a high-functioning individual with a thriving career, you'll need to step out of your comfort zone and face these difficult feelings head-on, otherwise, you'll carry them around with you all the time. For Meghan, dealing with discomfort meant learning to be more present and flexible. For you, it might mean learning to say no, taking a chance on a new relationship, having a tough conversation, or looking for a new (and better) job.

By flexing a little mindfulness, you'll be able to slow things down and sit with all that unease long enough to make the best decision instead of the decision that moves you away from discomfort quickly (but doesn't solve the problem). You'll also be better equipped to handle more future discomfort. The more you flex this muscle, the more prepared you will be for whatever life throws at you professionally or personally.

Making Friends with Discomfort

Embracing discomfort is not easy—if it were, it wouldn't be uncomfortable, right?—but knowing that you're working toward an achievement (a promotion, a job change, a healthier relationship) helps. People who weight-lift know: half the battle is mental. It can be tough to trust that you're making progress and that all the work is worth it. But then there comes a point where something clicks and you realize that your body is capable of *incredible* things if you can get out of your own way mentally. Suddenly, lifting the same amount of weight feels different . . . doable. The same is true of mindfulness. If you do the work for long enough, it will feel more doable, and you'll start to get out of your own way. To help you along, here are some key concepts that will help you reframe how to look at discomfort.

Mindfulness over Matter

Meditation is sometimes equated with mindfulness, but they are not the same. The practice of meditation—sitting with your thoughts in a quiet space—is a great *tool* for mindfulness. Why? Because it's uncomfortable. Who wants to be alone with their thoughts these days? But the more you practice it, the more it will increase your stamina to sit with discomfort. Just as working out at the gym prepares you to use your body in all kinds of ways in your regular life, meditation prepares you to withstand life's discomforts. I often tell my clients that meditation is the process of building a tiny house inside of yourself that is safe and calm. It takes years to create and needs continual maintenance, but once it's there, you can go and sit inside, accessing all the safety and calm you need anytime you need it.

Think about adding two to three minutes of meditation to your routine every morning. It may be hard to do at first, but if you stick with it, you'll notice that soon those two or three minutes will breeze by. At that point, increase your meditation time to whatever feels right for you. After a while, you'll start to notice that when you're uncomfortable in other parts of your life, you can drop into the space you've cultivated in your meditation practice for a quick reprieve.

YOU CAN TOLERATE MORE THAN YOU THINK.

Many people turn away from discomfort because they underesti-mate their tolerance for it. For example, I *hate* being physically un-comfortable. I'm that person who complains at the first twinge of a headache, who wears two sweaters in a chilly movie theater, and who worries when I get sick that I'll never feel better again. One day I asked myself why I am this way. After some reflection, I realized it came from being a sick infant. I spent a lot of time in physical pain and discomfort as a baby, and my poor young brain probably thought it would never end. I didn't develop trust that tough things pass. So for a long time as an adult, I did everything I could to avoid physical discomfort—I'd head inside if there was a chill in the air, skip the tough yoga class, and even avoid spicy food. But after missing out on one too many important or fun and healthy experiences, I asked myself if the things I was avoiding were really as bad as I thought they'd be. I decided to try leaning *toward* my discomfort instead of away from it. I reminded myself that my discomfort was temporary—that it would fade—and discovered my tolerance was stronger than I thought. And the benefits I felt when I tolerated my discomfort made it well worth the effort. I realized that often, it was the *worry about being uncomfortable forever* that stopped me from enjoying my-self, not the physical experience itself. And while I still don't love spicy foods, I can tolerate—even enjoy!—some salsa or a vindaloo curry once in a while.

Understanding that you can brave discomfort more than you think is a simple yet powerful mind shift. In my speaking engage-ments, I like to facilitate an exercise that illustrates this in real time. It's something that almost universally makes people a little uncom-fortable: an eye gaze. First, I ask the audience to partner up and stare directly into their partner's eyes for twenty-five seconds. I tell them they can blink but to try not to talk. Ready, set, go! In those precious seconds, I witness person after person do things to avoid their discomfort: they look away nervously, they laugh out loud, they say something to disarm the other person. In what seems like fifteen minutes to the audience, the twenty-five seconds are finally over. People laugh and breathe a sigh of relief, thinking the exercise is over.

I assure the audience that while it was natural to want to move away from their discomfort, the goal of the exercise is to show them that they're more capable of handling discomfort than they give themselves credit for. So I ask them to do the eye gaze again. After the groans and nervous laughter stop, I point out that this time, they have more information than they did before: they know what it will feel like, they know they can survive it, they know it won't last forever, and they know they're not in it alone. I tell them that this time, when they have the urge to look away or to laugh, to instead take a breath, stay present, and remind themselves that they can handle it.

In that second turn, there is always a *hugely* noticeable shift. The room is silent for twenty-five full seconds. No laughing or talking, just people being present with their partners. This time around, when the allotted twenty-five seconds are up, people are amazed. They did it. And many of them even *enjoyed* the moment of calm and presence. They often comment that the second round felt significantly shorter than the first round. I take this time to congratulate them and then ask them to remember this exercise and use the lessons learned whenever they are uncomfortable. It's a reminder that they can handle discomfort if they just breathe through it and that they'll come out on the other side having done something beautiful.

So the next time you're uncomfortable and want to move away from it, take a deep breath, feel your feelings, and remind yourself that, as Glennon Doyle says, you can do hard things. To help you do that, here are some prompts to use when you're feeling uncomfortable:

1. Try labeling your discomfort. What is it that's making the moment feel so intolerable? Where do you feel it in your body?

2. What is the worst thing that can happen? Play out the worst-case scenario. But then, and this is the important part, play out the *best*-case scenario and the *most likely* scenario as well.

3. Ask for support if you need it, and find comfort in the fact that you are not in it alone.

4. Remember that this feeling won't last forever; it is survivable.

5. Remind yourself that challenging this discomfort head-on is going to make you stronger and help you grow.

Whenever you're in an uncomfortable moment and you feel the urge to move away from it, pause and run through these reminders. They work for nearly any scenario: Need to have a difficult conversation with a teammate? Want to ask for a raise? Have to present in front of a large group of people? The more you do this, the easier and more intuitive it will become.

YOU CAN TURN BAD INTO GOOD.

Life is messy, and challenges inevitably come at us every day, week, and year. The struggle is real. On a 2022 episode of the podcast *Fly on the Wall* with Dana Carvey and David Spade, longtime *Saturday Night Live* producer Lorne Michaels talked about the challenges that befall all new members. He used the example of when Colin Jost and Michael Che, the longest-tenured "Weekend Update" anchors in *SNL* history, first started on the show. An NBC executive asked Michaels over dinner if he thought the "Weekend Update" segment was working.

"And I said no," Michaels shared.

"Oh, you *know* [it's not working]?" the executive replied.

"Yeah, it's a thing. . . . People have to be bad before they can be good."

In other words, you have to struggle through the bad and embrace the flubbed lines, missed cues, and performance anxiety to get through to the other side. Everything takes work and endurance.

But once you start, it gets easier. In his book *Atomic Habits*, James Clear prods readers to give themselves ten minutes for their bodies' endorphins to kick in when doing anything uncomfortable; that release of feel-good hormones will help you feel more at ease with the task at hand. You may think the run or swim will be painful, but once you hit the trail or pool and let those endorphins do their thing, you will feel great (or at least not horrible!). This applies to less intense versions of discomfort as well. In his book of short essays, *Peace Is Every Step*, Buddhist monk and prolific author Thich Nhat Hanh, describes the disparate discomfort of needing to do dishes with the often peaceful and enjoyable process of actually doing them.

Psychology also supports this: To overcome a phobia, anxiety, or other uncomfortable stimulus, a therapist might repeatedly expose you to it and challenge you to wait until your nervous system comes back to baseline. With each exposure, your body will respond less strongly, literally retraining how you tolerate the very things that make you uncomfortable. I remember when I first started doing public speaking gigs, the moment I got onstage my whole body would start shaking uncontrollably. It gave me some sense of why public speaking ranks above death for what people are most afraid of. I kept at it, though, over and over again, until getting on a stage no longer felt like a threat to my nervous system. I also learned what tools I need to feel confident and prepared: clear notes, enough (but not too much!) practice, and a comfortable pair of shoes. This repeated exposure to something that originally terrified me dulled my body's knee-jerk reaction, and these days, speaking in front of audiences of thousands no longer triggers any kind of stressful physiological response. It was a process, and it didn't happen overnight, but I got there. You can, too.

YOU CREATE YOUR OWN REALITY.

Sometimes tolerating discomfort is all about changing your perspective on it. Did you know that anxiety and excitement are very similar physiologically? And studies show flipping the two around in your mind can have profound impacts on your outlook: even simply reframing your thoughts as "I am excited" instead of "I am nervous" can change what your body sees as a threat into an opportunity. One of the best (and one of the hardest) things you can do on this road to emotional fitness is to learn how to acknowledge and live with multiple emotions at once, so this is a great opportunity to practice this. What if in addition to seeing risk you saw possibility? With panic, you felt excitement? Alongside doubt, you had curiosity?

If you can believe in the *possibility* of getting to where you want to go, then every decision you make is going to point you toward that possibility. At its core, this is what "manifesting" is all about. By pointing your compass intentionally toward your goals and feeling confident in your ability to get there, you increase the chances of achieving what you want. If you know you can handle hard things, then all the tiny unconscious choices you make daily will move you *toward* the things you want to achieve instead of *away* from the discomfort you might experience along the way.

Robin, an executive at a highly esteemed LA-based PR company, had more than twenty-five years of experience under her belt. While she loved the comfort of being at an established company, she was itching to go out on her own. Every week she talked to me about how exciting it would be to start her own agency. Every week she talked herself out of it. The idea of taking the leap terrified her.

"What should I do?" she wondered in my office one day. "How do I know if leaving is the right choice or not?"

"Well, first of all, maybe it's important to acknowledge that there might not be a *right* choice here. There are just choices. And no matter which choice you pick—staying at your company or leaving to start something new—you will gain things, and you will lose things. And losing things is always uncomfortable, so you're going to have to face that either way."

"You're right. But then . . . how do I know what choice to make?"

"Well, tell me about the part of you that wants to stay."

Robin told me it was nice to have a steady paycheck and that she worried about having to establish all new relationships in the industry if she left.

"That makes sense. Now tell me about the part of you that wants to go."

Robin's face lit up. She talked about how exhilarating it would be to be her own boss. She talked about the change she felt she could make in the industry. And she talked about how she'd always wanted to do something bold and audacious.

I reflected to Robin that her reasons for staying seemed to have more to do with fear than anything else, and I asked her what it might be like to build her life more around what brings her purpose and less around what soothes her fear. I asked her to write down a list of pros and cons before our next meeting. The next week, Robin said she was surprised at how long the pros column was compared to the cons and that the cons were much more about avoiding discomfort than moving toward her purpose. It helped her shift her anxiety into excitement. As we worked out steps to achieve her goal, what initially seemed unattainable became well within her grasp.

YOU CAN MAKE SMALL CHANGES THAT LEAD TO BIG TRANSFORMATIONS.

Changing your mindset isn't a quick fix. That first run will probably be excruciating. Let's say you wanted to be able to do one hundred push-ups. You're not going to start on day one doing one hundred—perhaps you'll do five or ten a day to start, gradually increasing the number. And after a few months, one hundred will feel doable. The same goes for your emotional fitness. If delegating work makes you uncomfortable, your first step wouldn't be to hand off your most important project, it would be to pry your fingers off your workload and delegate one small task to a colleague you trust.

While that step is an excellent move in the right direction, it's not the most important step in this process. That distinction is saved for step number two, where you take time for reflection. It's not your experiences but your reflection on your experiences that leads to change. Ask yourself: *What was it like to delegate that small task? Did I feel out of control? Did I feel worried that it wouldn't go well? Did I feel like I wasn't doing my job? How did it end up going? Was the outcome as bad as I worried it would be? What positives came out of leaning toward my discomfort?* Sit with those feelings, and see if, after some time, they carry any weight. Often, you'll realize that it wasn't so bad, and you'll be more likely to remember that the next time.

Sometimes, *not* doing something is uncomfortable. I like to tell my clients that if they want to understand why they do something, they should stop doing it and see how they feel. So if you want to know why you drink, smoke, shop, eat, or gamble more than you'd like to, stop the behavior and see what feelings come up. You're probably doing these things to avoid uncomfortable emotions or truths. Similarly, when you want to get better at being uncomfortable, do something that makes you uncomfortable and then reflect on it. What are you feeling? What worries came up for you? What is it that you're trying to avoid? Once you know the underlying issues, then you can work on them. In other words, be present with your discomfort and try to understand why something makes you uncomfortable in the first place. Upon such reflection, you will learn from it and have more ability to move through it.

I once worked with a tech designer named Jamie. He felt undervalued and underpaid at work, but something stopped him from standing up for himself and asking for a raise. He struggled with confrontation, especially with authority, so he couldn't seem to work up the nerve to walk into his boss's office. As we worked together, it came out that he grew up in a fairly stoic family in which no one voiced their feelings or needs, and issues were quietly ignored or swept under the rug. If he ever told his parents he was frustrated or upset, they told him to toughen up and deal with it. A part of him knew this wasn't the best way to deal with problems, but he was never taught another way.

I saw this behavior play out in our therapy sessions as well. In one of our meetings, it came out that Jamie had been wishing we could change our session time for months, but he'd never brought it up. He told me he assumed it would be inconvenient for me, but I knew it was a deeply entrenched desire to avoid any sort of confrontation. I called him out on it (gently).

"Well, Jamie, this feels important to talk about because it's showing up in other places. You prioritized your assumption about what I would feel over your own needs, and it's kept you from getting what you wanted—the time slot you wanted has been available this whole time."

We used the opportunity to talk through his discomfort with asking for his needs to be met and explored how he could advocate for himself. We also spent time exploring what might live on the other side of this discomfort. Jaime talked about how nice it would be if he could confront things more directly at work. We thought about the worst-case scenario if he asked for a raise and realized it wouldn't be any worse than the situation he was already in. And we practiced having him locate where he felt the discomfort in his body so he could take a few breaths and center himself before pushing forward. Eventually, he felt empowered enough to schedule the meeting with his boss, who gave him an even higher raise than he asked for.

YOU DON'T ALWAYS HAVE TO "TRUST YOUR GUT."

Your discomfort does serve a purpose, and mindfulness doesn't mean ignoring it completely. Sometimes your discomfort is telling you to proceed with caution for good reason. Uncomfortable walking down that dark alley by yourself at night? It's probably smart to heed that inner warning. So how do you know when to move toward your discomfort and when to use it as a sign that you should avoid something? Often people will say that you should "always trust your gut." This old motto has been around for centuries, but it's not great advice. Here's why: your gut instinct tells you what it thinks will keep you safe. While it can be a wonderful strategy to help you make quick decisions or tune into something that could be dangerous, it's often formed from trauma and bias instead of truth.

For example, if you were bitten by a dog as a kid, your gut instinct around all dogs might be that they're dangerous. Or let's say you grew up in a culture that perceives a particular group of people as lazy. This unconscious bias—a subconscious preference based on past experiences or perceptions—may come into play in your decision-making. While interviewing employee candidates, you may overlook someone because of this bias, denying you and your company a highly qualified applicant who could be a huge asset to your company.

This shows up in your personal life as well. I had a client, Camilla, who was abused emotionally by her parents growing up. As an adult, she had a string of unhealthy relationships, and after much therapy, we discovered that part of her believed that she did not deserve to be treated with love and respect because she wasn't treated that way as a child. After a lot of hard work, she found herself in a loving relationship where she was treated with compassion and kindness. End of story, right? Wrong. In a session a few months into this relationship, she told me she felt so confused—she was trying to decide whether to stay in the relationship, and when she asked people about it, everyone told her to "trust her gut." The problem was, her gut was screaming at her to run! It told her that she didn't deserve the relationship, that her new partner was too good for her, and that she should leave before he figured it out. Camilla had to use her rational mind to have a conversation with her gut instinct. She had to figure out if her gut was leading her toward the life she wanted to live or if, in trying to protect her, it was actually keeping her from growing.

I'm not telling you this to encourage you to ignore your intuition. You should listen to your instincts, of course, because sometimes they do keep you safe, but they also may stop you from living life differently than you have in the past. With Camilla, we dug a little deeper. In one session, I asked to talk to her younger self.

"How old is this part of you that feels you don't deserve love and respect?"

"I don't know, I think about eight?"

"Okay, let me have a conversation with your eight-year-old self. Young Camilla, what do you think adult Camilla should do here?"

"Well, I think she should leave this relationship because it's going too well, and I don't deserve that." Aha. There it was.

"Now, let's bring your older, wiser self into the conversation. How would she talk to your eight-year-old self?"

"Okay . . . here goes: Young Me, I know it's hard to imagine that you deserve better because you didn't get it when you needed it the most. But you *do* deserve better, and I'm going to make sure you get it."

Once we knew where her struggles were coming from, we could work on them. So remember that your gut is not a source of infallible truth and you should listen with discernment, explore what comes up, and make well-informed decisions based on both instinct and reason.

Remember how I told you I hated physical discomfort? I eventually became aware that this was based on outdated instinct and it wasn't working for me anymore, especially when I felt I was missing out on meaningful experiences. So, in these moments, I practiced checking in with myself and asking, *This feeling I am having that seems unbearable . . . is it* actually *unbearable? Or is it telling me that because there's this sick infant inside me who worries that it'll never get better?* If it's the latter, I can rationalize that I'm okay, breathe through it, and lean toward the discomfort instead of away from it.

YOU CAN ADOPT NEW COPING PATTERNS.

Figuring out your coping patterns is a big step in changing your default reactions and adopting a better approach. Give yourself time. Sitting with that feeling for a few minutes while breathing normally, you will see there is less to fear than you think. Being present with your discomfort *compounds* your growth. On *Arnold's Pump Club*, podcast host and bodybuilding icon Arnold Schwarzenegger explains that he doesn't listen to music while working out. He wants to be present with what he's putting his body through, not distract himself from it. When you're mindful, you no longer need to break every uncomfortable silence, fix every nagging issue, or avoid every difficult conversation. Each time you sit with your discomfort successfully, your capacity to tolerate it will incrementally increase, and you will develop this into a healthier coping pattern you can use anytime. Once Meghan and I understood that uncertainty made her uncomfortable, we worked on ways to help her. For instance, when there was a moment of silence in our session and I could see her tense up, I would ask her calmly if we might stay together in the silence for a moment to show her she was capable of handling the discomfort.

"What are you feeling now?" I'd ask.

"Ugh. My heart is racing, and I have a tight knot in my stomach."

This was her fight-or-flight response in action—that impulse that tells her she needs to do something in reaction to a perceived threat (in her case, silence). So, in those moments when I'd notice Meghan start to get fidgety and anxious, I would ask her to take a slow breath and sit through it. I also took a breath to show I was in the moment with her.

Her heart rate would inevitably slow and she would feel relieved to get through the discomfort in one piece, and each time we did this, it became less and less intolerable. Together, we worked on building her mindfulness to the point that she could let a conversation *breathe*. From there, she practiced living more in the moment, trusting the process without a step-by-step plan.

As she learned to do that, a few major things shifted. For one, she was more successful in her job. Meghan's close rate went up as she learned to give potential customers time to absorb information and ask questions before giving an answer. It turns out, people respond better to a more collaborative sales pitch than to one that leaves them feeling strong-armed into a decision they're not ready to make. Any unease Meghan felt about not pressing for an answer was alleviated as she started to see the results of this new tactic in her monthly sales reports. Her superiors agreed: Meghan's boss, Talia, let her know that colleagues and customers alike felt more supported because Meghan was becoming more collaborative and less demanding.

This changed outside the office, too—her fraying friendships started to heal as she was no longer trying to micromanage every get-together with her circle of friends. Sitting in temporary discomfort (such as waiting for someone to reply to a text or being patient as her friends came to a consensus on dinner plans) was a small price to pay for the closer relationships she started to forge. I noticed a shift in our therapy sessions as well. Rather than coming in having written a script in advance (something she did on more than one occasion!), Meghan started arriving at my office with no set agenda and, instead, let thoughts and feelings guide her. We could be more imaginative—even creative—together. At the end of one session, she remarked, "Wow, I didn't even realize I needed to talk about that."

"Yup, that happens when you don't have an ironclad plan."

While I wouldn't say Meghan ever came to *love* uncertainty, she got better at tolerating it, and she felt the benefits ripple through her life: entire days went by without a single social gaffe. Respect and acknowledgment for her and her work grew throughout the organization. And most important, she felt better about how she was showing up in her relationships and in her life—all because she built the strength to breathe through her discomfort.

YOU CAN TRUST YOUR FUTURE SELF.

No one is immune to feeling uncomfortable with the unknown, not even us therapists. But I have learned that your "future self" has your back. I learned this lesson many years ago when my mom was in the hospital for about a month. Things looked dire for the first few weeks, and at the time it didn't look like she would make it. I was on a roller coaster of anxiety and anticipatory grief.

One particularly tough night at the hospital, a family friend, Bill, came by. He was an oncologist, so he had a lot of experience with families facing hard decisions, impending loss, and grief. I was grateful to see a familiar face, and as I sat next to him on a bench outside my mom's room, he asked how I was doing. I admitted, "Honestly, I'm terrified. I don't know what I'll do if my mom dies." I was still at an age when losing a parent seemed unfathomable. I continued: "I don't think I'll be able to handle it, like I'll just completely fall apart." Tears streamed down my face as I faced the terror of losing my mom.

Bill, a tall man with kind eyes, looked at me and said, "Emily, the version of you that will handle that terrible thing if and when it happens, will be born into existence in that moment. And that version of you will have more life experience, more information, and more capacity to handle that terrible thing than you do now. It makes sense that present you doesn't know how you'd handle it, because the version of you that will handle it doesn't exist yet! But future you will figure it out. You have to trust your future self to handle future problems. What you're going through right now is already so painful. And you know as hard as it is, you're handling it. You might not have known in the past how you'd get through this moment, but present you is figuring it out, and present you needs to trust that future you will do the same."

Now this just completely blew my mind. This idea that I should trust my future self made so much sense to me, and it released the burden of trying to figure how to handle something that hadn't even happened yet. This advice helped me through that terrible moment, and it's helped me get through other really tough moments.

But I also draw on it for smaller, everyday moments of anxiety. Anytime I think, *What will I do if I get sick? Or if I fail at a project? Or if I miss the bus?* I remind myself, *Future me is a badass, she will figure it out.* Anxiety is suffering future pain, often unnecessarily, so by trusting your future self, you will prevent yourself a lot of unnecessary struggle. (By the way, my mom made it out of the hospital, and I was grateful that I hadn't spent too much time and energy trying to solve a problem that didn't come to be.)

Learning to trust your future self can form the bedrock of a mindful, in-the-moment approach to facing life's challenges. By developing the inner capacity to turn *toward* different kinds of discomfort instead of away from them, you will start to gain a sense of ownership over your own life. And even more important, by flexing these muscles, you are building your body up for the hard work that is to come in all the following chapters; just like at the gym, you need to lean into the discomfort and do the hard work, or it isn't going to do squat for you.

The Mindfulness Push-Up: The Shock Absorber

It's time to practice getting more comfortable being uncomfortable. This push-up is all about increasing your tolerance for discomfort.

> **STEP 1:** Think of one thing that makes you a little uncomfortable. It doesn't have to be something that terrifies you, just something you tend to avoid. Maybe it's saying no or providing constructive criticism to a coworker, maybe it's opening up about yourself to new people, or maybe it's holding warrior pose in a yoga class.

> **STEP 2:** Explore the worry that lives beneath the discomfort. Underneath discomfort with saying no might be a worry that you won't be liked. Beneath discomfort asking for a raise might be worry about rejection. By identifying what you're *really* trying to avoid, you'll be able to make a more informed choice about the situation.

> **STEP 3:** Think about what you tend to do to avoid this particular type of discomfort. Maybe saying no makes you uncomfortable so you say yes too often, even when you don't want to. Or perhaps being the center of attention makes you queasy, so you deflect the spotlight onto other people. Think about how this avoidance might actually *create* more problems for you than facing the original discomfort would.

> **STEP 4:** Think of a shock absorber. A shock absorber is anything that helps you tolerate the discomfort in some way and lean into it instead of away from it. For example, instead of

saying yes when you *really* mean no, you could say, "Hmm, let me think about that." That way, you give yourself time to figure out how to say no properly. Or if you tend to avoid public speaking, maybe practice giving a talk in the mirror or to a friend to get a little more comfortable with it. Sometimes a shock absorber is as simple as taking three slow breaths before you take action.

STEP 5: Lean into your discomfort! You don't have to get too extreme here; you're going for slight discomfort, not pain or panic. But with the help of your shock absorber, show yourself that you are capable of doing that tough thing you were hesitant to tackle. You can take the smallest of steps at a time, but make a regular practice of it. With consistent effort, this should cultivate the mindfulness demanded by the rest of this program. And the better you are at tolerating discomfort, the more options you'll have available to you.

In the poem "Diving Board," the brilliant Shel Silverstein wrote about a young boy scared to dive off a diving board. As he teeters on the edge, he does everything he can think of to avoid actually taking the plunge: he makes sure that the board has just enough bounce, that its spring is tight, and that his toes have the proper grip . . . he is "Doin' everything . . . but DIVE." The beauty of this poem is that it perfectly captures all that is uncomfortable with the unknown, the new, and the awkward, and how that can lead to inaction and deprive us of living our best selves. And while learning to tolerate the unknown is crucial, learning as much about yourself as possible is equally important. To do that, you'll need to ask yourself some difficult questions and be ready for some equally difficult answers. Ready to dive in? Good, let's plunge into **curiosity.**

4

CURIOSITY
Pursuing Growth

I have no special talents. I am only passionately curious.

—ALBERT EINSTEIN

At first, Steven succeeded precisely *because* of his lack of curiosity.

Working like crazy to get his ambitious start-up off the ground, Steven ignored everyone's feedback: investors telling him his idea was far-fetched, friends worried he was risking too much, and internet trolls tearing him down (Steven's sizable social media presence helped his business grow but also made him a target for online abuse).

Unlike most aspiring entrepreneurs, Steven didn't need anyone telling him to "ignore the haters." That was just his way. He pushed right through setbacks and negative feedback that might have derailed a more open and vulnerable individual. As a result, Steven grew his B2B software company into a thriving outfit with thousands of customers, dozens of employees, and rapidly ballooning profits.

But soon, cracks opened inside and out. Outside, Steven's employees, customers, and investors grew so frustrated with Steven's tendency to ignore them that it threatened to topple everything he'd worked so hard to build. Inside, Steven became anxious and depressed for reasons he didn't understand. Success made him struggle like failure never could. Only two years after founding his start-up and having built enough success to dread losing it, Steven came to me for help.

Talking with Steven and seeing how defensive and buttoned-up he was, I knew working with him would be a challenge. However, in his reaching out for help, I saw at least a spark of the curiosity he would need to make change happen. On some level, Steven had finally started wondering why he always shut himself off from other people. Intellectually, he knew he ought to listen to others and connect with them, to some extent, anyway, but something inside him resisted. In my experience, most people don't go to therapy because they don't know what to do. They go to therapy because they *do* know what to do but need help understanding why they're not doing it.

From the start, I was struck by Steven's self-confidence. He didn't seem to care what anybody thought about him. From the beginning of his career, he'd demonstrated an almost unnerving capacity to push past *no*.

"I've listened to my instincts my entire life," he said. "Other people just want to destroy my success. Why would I listen to them?"

As a society, we tend to admire, even idolize, stubborn and self-directed individuals like Steven—if their efforts lead to success. This admiration is even more profound among Steven's world of entrepreneurs and in the progress-at-any-cost arena of Silicon Valley. What I learned in our sessions, however, was that this obstinance didn't come naturally. Steven worked hard to stay disconnected from others' ideas and opinions. Unsurprisingly, this tendency showed up with me in the therapy room. Whenever I invited him to think about a situation differently or offered gentle reflection about how his behaviors might affect others, he played defense. At one point, he expressed anger toward his right-hand man, John, who had offered to take a time-consuming project off his plate. Steven had scoffed at the offer; he was sure his partner wanted to undermine him.

"Is it hard to imagine that he might just have wanted to support you?" I asked once I had a moment to interject. But before my words could sink in, before he could feel them, he began cataloging the reasons I was wrong.

"You give people *way* too much credit. And if you think that way, I'm not sure how you're going to be able to help me."

I let the comment go, as it was clear in that early session that Steven wasn't ready to take in my feedback. Still, the interaction helped me understand the way Steven's Teflon-coated ego was keeping him defiantly alone, trapped in his own world, oblivious to why his behaviors were problematic for himself and his company.

Steven's outright and habitual dismissal of the needs and opinions of others meant that nothing could get in his way—except himself. Starved of the feedback that might make him a better leader, let alone a better human being, he increasingly alienated the very people he needed to get his business to the next level. Often, employees, customers, and investors were wrong about what needed to happen. But sometimes, they *did* have something valuable to contribute. Unfortunately, this highly guarded founder didn't listen, let alone distinguish good input from bad.

When smart and talented people convince themselves that they've succeeded by ignoring the doubts of others, they become oppositional by default. They can't even hear you telling them to listen. In discounting the haters, Steven was missing out on invaluable feedback from employees with good ideas, experienced investors charting a path to an acquisition, and loyal customers flagging areas for improvement. Since nothing that violated his worldview registered with him, Steven was stuck and didn't know why.

"You're prioritizing revenue over quality," one investor told him. "I've seen this pattern with other companies at this stage, and it doesn't end well. I recommend you slow down and go back to basics. Would you like my help?"

As you might guess, Steven's answer was an immediate no.

"If that investor really knew what he was doing," Steven told me, "he'd be running his own company." The decision to decline help ended up costing him dearly. As Steven's company progressed, his default stance of defensiveness over growth had gone from a useful strength to a profound weakness. To his great detriment, Steven had deliberately shut off his curiosity. As I got to know him better, it became clear why.

Growing up, Steven had existed in a total vacuum of outside support. His father was physically present but emotionally absent, a doormat. His mother, in contrast, was an intense, aggressive woman who struggled with alcoholism and took any opportunity to force unwanted advice down her son's throat. Getting nothing he needed from one parent and nothing he wanted from the other, Steven became his own support system. Gifted and driven, he looked out for himself so successfully as a young man that he became convinced that he would never need anyone else.

It's a testament to Steven's resilience and natural talents (and a healthy dose of privilege) that, despite his unwillingness to ask for help, he attended an Ivy League school, earned an MBA, and launched a successful career in tech. Steven got support along the way from friends, teachers, and relatives, of course, but none of that ever felt like support to him because he didn't ask for it, and he didn't let himself expect it. Rather than experience frightening feelings of dependence, his mind worked nonstop to convince itself that every significant step was taken solo. This defensive habit of thought made Steven feel safe. However, it also left him brittle. Over time, shielding this false sense of independence became more and more important to his well-being.

Strengths tend to become weaknesses when we don't keep an eye on them. Like other aspects of emotional fitness, the trait that had gotten Steven through tough times now stood between him and the life he wanted. Whether at work or in his relationships, Steven automatically deflected the things he most needed to hear. Friendships wilted. Romantic relationships went nowhere. Women who found themselves attracted to Steven's competence and independence met the "other Steven" as soon as he liked them enough to feel remotely dependent—that's when he pulled away for dear life. Emotionally absent like his father, and critical and defensive like his mother, Steven possessed all the skills he needed to remain blissfully autonomous . . . and alone.

It may seem strange to think of curiosity as a strength that can be developed alongside traits like mindfulness or communication. You're either curious or you're not, right? And even if curiosity were something you could somehow increase, what's left to be curious about? So much information is at our fingertips that we rarely stop and give ourselves the time to sit with curiosity. Technology and AI algorithms have been tweaked to anticipate our every need. And when you do have a question, the answer you seek is a few clicks away—*Is it going to rain in fifteen minutes?* (Google says yes.) *Who should I date?* (Your last few swipes offer some options.) *How am I feeling today?* (Your horoscope app warns that Mercury retrograde means you'll struggle to be productive.)

People also confuse curiosity with being intrusive—they see curious people as inquisitive, nosy busybodies. Overdo curiosity, and you get on other people's nerves with all your prying questions. But the curiosity you'll train up in this chapter has nothing to do with unwelcome digging into other people's secrets. Instead, it's about opening up to what is being willingly offered to you. Our second trait of emotional fitness, curiosity, is the pursuit of understanding and growth over defensiveness. It's the capacity to ask yourself tough questions, face difficult realities, and not only hear but *listen* when people give you feedback. Prioritizing growth over comfort, you'll practice taking everything in, good and bad, evaluating it bravely, asking questions, learning what you can, and leaving the rest.

The Fortress We Build

We all go to great lengths to protect ourselves from uncomfortable truths or emotions—about others, and especially about ourselves. Just as a king would build a fortress to protect his kingdom from intruders, we each build a fortress to protect ourselves from per- ceived threats around us (and within us). Every time we go through something difficult, we put a brick in the wall to try to keep it from happening again. The human mind is intricate and multifaceted, with thoughts, emotions, and experiences that are deeply intercon- nected, and our first instinct is often to armor up. If you've ever been hurt in a romantic relationship and then been a bit hypervigilant or paranoid that the exact same thing was going to happen in your next relationship, you understand what I'm talking about.

But this self-protective instinct can also cause gaps in aware- ness. Just like a blind spot in a car obstructs your view, a blind spot in your psyche will keep you from seeing things you need to con- front and change. Peeking behind the wall of your fortress may stir up painful feelings. Or maybe it would necessitate some difficult work you'd rather not embark on. I can't tell you how many of my clients completely ignore how stressed they are because they're not ready to face the fact that their work, their relationship, or their life choices are unhealthy (and would thus need to change). In other words, curiosity can be uncomfortable, which is why you've got to keep flexing those mindfulness muscles from chapter 3. Remember, each of these seven skills builds on the others, just as all the muscles in your body are interconnected.

PLAYING DEFENSE

In a physical confrontation, you would likely put up your hands to protect yourself—similarly, in emotional situations, you might feel the need to verbally protect yourself. No one wants to hear that they're failing or flailing. So, when someone tells you that you made a mistake, what do you do? You might reply with overly apologetic excuses ("I am *so sorry* the Q4 projections were late! My internet went down, then my computer froze, and then . . ."), you might deflect ("The numbers I received from sales were off, so I had to double-check all the numbers myself."), or you might openly deny the problem ("Well, I emailed them to you last night, maybe you deleted the email by accident."). In other words, you might get defensive.

Defense mechanisms are mental processes that we use to avoid conflict or anxiety, and they are largely unconscious (meaning we don't even realize they're happening). Your defenses are the bricks in your fortress: they help you feel safe, but they can also prevent you from seeing important truths. We are all naturally defensive sometimes, but at some point, you must learn to understand and tolerate the difference between what you *want* to be true and what *is* true. How do you do it? You guessed it . . . the answer is curiosity.

Being curious is the opposite of being defensive. Rather than fighting to keep uncomfortable information out, you're actively asking to take it in. And that generally involves asking a lot of questions (both to yourself and to others), figuring out the whys, and learning how to do better next time. (*Why was I late in getting the Q4 projections done on time? What was I really avoiding? How could I approach things differently in the future?*) Curiosity helps you think more strategically, have more collaborative relationships, and increase trust. It helps you discern when your defenses are protecting you, and when they're getting in your way. Without it, it will be nearly impossible to grow, improve, or evolve.

Let's take a look at several common defense mechanisms by which you might be avoiding emotional discovery, and how to get curious instead.

1) *"You're* the one with the problem.": Projection. You might assume you know how people feel or why they do or say something, but those assumptions might actually say more about you than they do about them. Projection is an unconscious response where you attribute emotions, thoughts, or motives to other people that you don't want to face in yourself. Think of a jealous romantic partner who accuses you of being unfaithful to avoid facing their own desire to cheat. But no one wants to take responsibility for someone else's feelings, and by learning to own what you yourself feel, you'll judge others' motivations and behaviors more accurately.

Try this:
Instead of saying, "You're the problem" . . . ask yourself: *How might I be contributing to this problem?*

2) "This company is the problem.": Institutional transference. When you put feelings about something from your

personal life into an institution you're associated with (such as the company you work for), it's called institutional transference. Institutional transference is similar to projection in that you are misplacing the feelings you have about one thing onto something else, but here we are talking about external forces, not internal ones. For example, let's say you feel unsupported by leadership at work—they haven't been looking out for the interests of you and your colleagues. It might feel unacceptable to be angry with your company because finding a new job would be difficult, so you might put that anger somewhere that feels more acceptable. For example, you might start to feel your partner is being unsupportive out of nowhere. You may even start a fight or argue or feel hopeless or angry with your partner, all the while having no idea that your feelings are about something else entirely.

Try this:
Instead of assuming that one person, situation, or institution is the cause of your frustration . . . ask yourself: *Where else in my life might this feeling belong?*

3) "If I ignore the problem, it'll go away.": Avoidance. Just as you might put off a benign task—laundry, paperwork, working out—you might also push away feelings or experiences that you perceive as distressing or anxiety-inducing. As we discussed earlier, it's normal to want to protect yourself from discomfort or emotional pain. But guess what? *What you resist persists.* The emotions you don't let yourself feel and the thoughts you don't let yourself think become burdens that you will carry around with you in every moment. Are you ignoring feelings of anger or sadness because you're hoping they'll just disappear? Your feelings will find a way to be known, and until you face them head-on, they will grow in strength against you.

Try this:
Instead of avoiding a problem or feeling and hoping it goes away . . . ask yourself: *Why am I avoiding this feeling? What's so uncomfortable about it? How can I set some time aside to lean into it (for example, putting on some sad music and crying it out)?*

4) "I'll show you a problem!": Acting out. When you can't acknowledge that you feel something, it will show up in your behavior. If you're unhappy about having to attend a boring meeting because you're overwhelmed at work, you might show up late or unprepared. If you're feeling angry at a friend but don't want to confront them, you might forget to call them on their birthday. Your mind works on many levels, including levels you are not aware of. By improving your ability to recognize and own your feelings, you will reduce the likelihood that you act in ways that you regret or that go against your values.

Try this:
Instead of showing someone you're upset in a passive-aggressive way . . . ask yourself: *How do I really feel about this behavior?* Then have a direct conversation with them about what happened, how it made you feel, and what you'd like to see change the next time.

5) "I understand the problem, so I don't need to feel it.": Intellectualization. Here's a tough pill to swallow for many people—*you can't think your way out of a feeling.* Intellectualization involves distancing yourself from a distressing situation by focusing on its rational aspects. This can give you a sense of control, especially if you're more comfortable using your mind than sitting in tough emotions. I see this all the time with my ambitious tech clients, who are used to thinking their way through problems. Instead of acknowledging their emotional struggles, they focus on the details and try to use logic to fix things. While this intellectualization may help them in the short term, avoiding underlying emotional issues can lead to burnout in the long term.

Try this:
Instead of endlessly thinking about a problem . . . ask yourself: *How do I actually* feel *about this problem?*

6) "I *love* this problem.": Reaction formation. Have you ever noticed yourself acting overly nice to someone you don't like? This is a reaction formation: a common way to cope with inner conflicts and reduce anxiety by acting the opposite way to how you actually feel. Ever have a colleague with a distinctly narcissistic air about him? He may actually be masking feelings of insecurity and self-doubt. This one can be taken to extremes as well—I see news stories every day about people who are caught doing things they have seemingly devoted their whole lives to condemning. From politicians who feign morality but are then caught in compromising situations to body-positivity celebrities being called out on their own bullying behavior, it's more common than you think.

Try this:

Instead of telling someone that everything is okay when it definitely isn't . . . ask yourself: *How do I actually feel about this situation? Why might I be nervous to own or share those feelings?*

7) "All you are is a problem.": Splitting. Splitting is a tendency to see people, situations, or even yourself in extremes of all good or all bad, with little or no shades of gray. For example, during the "honeymoon phase" of your relationship, you might idealize your partner, seeing them as perfect and infallible. Then, as soon as any flaws or conflicts arise, you might quickly switch to viewing them as entirely negative and intolerable, leading to a turbulent relationship or breakup. This mindset keeps you from having to tolerate the fact that nothing is all good or all bad; the fantasy is that you can just avoid the bad things and go toward the good things. But you have to accept that there's good and bad in everything.

Try this:

Instead of seeing an issue, a person, or a situation as black-or-white . . . ask yourself: *How can I find the gray?* For example, if you find yourself thinking that your colleague is terrible in every way, challenge yourself to make a list of their positive attributes.

8) "I already know you're going to be a problem.": Bias. Bias generally refers to the preconceived perspectives, opinions, and assumptions we form based on our upbringing, culture, and society. At its core, bias is a protective mechanism, but it can be hugely problematic when left unexamined. You might want to group people or things because it makes it simpler to understand the world. It is also tempting to "blame" some other person or group of people rather than accepting the role you play in your own frustrations. For example, if you feel powerless in a society, you might try to find a group of people to blame and convince yourself that if you just got rid of this group, all your problems would go with them. At work, this can look like demonizing a certain person or group of people ("The sales team doesn't care about the success of this company.").

Try this:
Instead of assuming your ideas about a person or situation are true . . . ask yourself: *Why might I think this way?* For example, *Do I dislike all salespeople because all salespeople are really bad? Or because I've had issues with a few salespeople in the past?*

There are many other ways you protect yourself from uncomfortable truths, but these are a few to keep an eye out for. You may be a mastermind at hiding things from yourself, but the more you learn, the more you'll face head-on, and the more you'll be able to live your life with intention. Just by acknowledging that you see the world through a particular lens that's clouded by your own biases and experiences, you are being "meta-cognitive"—which means thinking about your thinking—and it's a great step toward seeing things more clearly. By getting curious, you can ask yourself, *Am I seeing things as they really are? Or is there more here that I should understand?*

WHY AREN'T WE CURIOUS?

The reason curiosity comes after mindfulness is because it is a deeply uncomfortable practice. When you act defensively instead of with curiosity, it's usually because you're afraid of something. It's your instinct kicking you into survival mode—your primitive mind is telling you to run for shelter and take cover. For people with severely untapped curiosity, opening an email that might contain a piece of unwelcome news feels almost life-threatening. They end up with inboxes spilling over with important information, not just bad news growing worse through negligence but also good opportunities that have long since expired.

Your environment can come into play as well. Family, society, and the workplace may have taught you to protect yourself fiercely and to be reticent to ask "too many questions," especially at a well-established company that says, "This is how we do it here." You might avoid being curious without even realizing it by surrounding yourself with people who agree with you. For leaders, this can look like hiring yes-men and women who never push back or question things. Leaders like this aren't deliberately sabotaging themselves. They genuinely think they are right because those loyal employees always say yes.

Look around: Do you only listen to those who agree with you? I bet you do it at least occasionally in your personal life: When you're dealing with a challenging situation, do you go to the friend who will give you the advice you *want* to hear (ahem, he or she tells you how great you are) rather than hard advice you *need* to hear? If so, you're not alone.

These emotional walls you build are trying to protect three things: A sense of feeling **safe**, a sense of being a **good** person, and a sense of **belonging**. In a moment of frustrated honesty, an employee blurts out, "I don't feel like you listen to me." The busy manager doesn't want to hear this because it conflicts with their self-image as a "good boss." Rather than take it in, they deflect: "You need to do a better job communicating." Or "I hear your ideas, but they just aren't as good as they need to be." With one sentence, that manager has thrown away a huge opportunity to improve. Likely, you can relate to both sides of this encounter.

I myself have had plenty of work to do on lowering my natural defenses: At the beginning of my career as a therapist, I found it difficult to receive feedback on my work, whether from my clients, supervisors, or peers. When they told me what I might do better, it *felt* like they were saying I was a bad therapist and always would be. We all need to feel like we're "good," and I wanted to be a "good therapist." To defend myself from this unpleasant feeling, I would dismiss the feedback that would one day make me the competent therapist I'd always wanted to be.

I remember a time my supervisor reviewed one of my sessions with a client as a teaching exercise and pointed out my tendency to let the client jump horizontally across topics rather than help him dig down into a single area where he might find some clarity. All I could hear from this useful feedback was: *You don't have what it takes. You've let your client down.* Rather than let my supervisor's words sink in, I got defensive, arguing that I'd simply followed the client's lead. Scrambling for excuses, I kept making the case that I'd done exactly what I was supposed to do, as though I knew better than my supervisor. By responding to honest feedback this way, I shut myself off from a crucial piece of learning.

In wanting to see myself as good, I kept myself from getting better.

If I'd made the flip to curiosity instead, asking my supervisor for specific examples from the session where I might have gone more vertical, I'd have learned something valuable and progressed more quickly.

LOWERING THE DRAWBRIDGE

With Steven's story, you may be reminded of another tech entrepreneur, coincidentally also named Steve, famous for ignoring the haters and doing things his way. Even a cursory read of contemporary accounts will reveal, however, that Steve Jobs was perfectly capable of hearing and acting on feedback from other people. Yes, one had to demonstrate serious competence and confidence to earn this willingness to listen, but there is no question that Jobs's curiosity amplified his accomplishments. I often wonder if he had developed this capacity further, whether he would have had a more well-rounded personal life to match his professional success.

With my client Steven, I relied on observation between us to help him see some truths about himself: "You know, Steven, I notice when I push back on you here, you tell me all the reasons I'm wrong instead of taking a moment to think about what I've said and asking for clarity about what I mean," I told him.

"I was just explaining my position," he replied the first time I pointed this out, reaching for the same deflecting behavior. "I'm not shutting you down."

"Hmm . . . can you feel that you're doing it right now?" I asked. "I imagine what I'm saying feels a little uncomfortable or painful to hear."

By labeling Steven's defensive behavior in the moment like this every time it cropped up, I helped cue him to rebuild his willingness to listen. His curiosity. Eventually, Steven learned to pause in those moments and consider what I was offering, even if it was uncomfortable, and he accepted the idea that by protecting himself from the opinions of others, he only exacerbated the problems those opinions might have helped him resolve. If you don't feel it, you can't heal it. Over time, Steven took up the metaphor of a king in a castle to convey his dawning realization. He told me that he had built a moat full of crocodiles out of necessity, but that had left him stuck in his castle, protected but lonely.

It took some time, but Steven began to feel safe with me—he learned to trust that I wasn't going to bark orders like his mother or ignore him like his father. And he began to see the benefit of having someone to think with. Best of all, he learned to lean into the discomfort that would spur personal growth. And once Steven was fully convinced of the value of curiosity in his life, he started practicing it as diligently as he had the other core skills of an entrepreneur. Learning how to negotiate a deal or speak in public was necessary in his career. Curiosity was just one more muscle to build.

When employees came to him with feedback, Steven consciously and deliberately resisted the urge to shut them down. To short-circuit this well-honed, instinctive response, he would ask question after question instead, digging deeper to avoid pulling away. Even as he experienced annoyance, discomfort, or even anger, he would press forward, asking for more of the same. What surprised Steven most was not how greatly he benefited from what he was finally able to hear, but rather how people started stepping closer to him in ways he never realized he had craved. Once he'd lowered the drawbridge, people began entering the castle. This strengthened his friendships, led to a meaningful romantic connection, and unleashed his leadership potential.

When a major tech company expressed interest in acquiring Steven's business, we worked together on ways to conduct the conversation collaboratively instead of adversarially. Steven's defenses screamed, "I don't need them." Thanks to his hard work, however, he could counter this protective instinct by accepting that he *wanted* this for himself, as terrifying as that was to feel. The boy who had learned to crave perfect autonomy became the man who accepted the imperfect fact that we all need others from time to time. Learning to be curious led directly to the eight-figure sale of Steven's company.

Steven's story may have spurred some self-reflection in you. Perhaps you're thinking that some of the defenses you developed during childhood, defenses that protected you from difficult feelings when escape wasn't an option, have now become a liability. For example, if you grew up in a home with physical or emotional abuse, you may have learned to make yourself small and quiet to avoid getting hurt. Now that you're out of that situation, you may still keep your head down even as life's opportunities pass you by. Or, if you grew up in a home where you were constantly criticized, as Steven did, you may have learned to ignore what others say about you by convincing yourself that you don't really care. Or perhaps you went the other direction and are incredibly sensitive to people's thoughts about you.

If you can even just recognize and acknowledge where in your life you are defensive, you're doing great. This is mindfulness and curiosity at work. No one is completely free of defensiveness. But you can learn to examine feedback in the moment and sit with the discomfort long enough to ask: *Am I protecting myself or keeping myself from learning what I need to know?* Labeling it whenever you find yourself shutting down interrupts that unconscious mechanism and helps eliminate it. But to let go of your outdated, counterproductive defensive blueprint, you will have to get some reps in.

THE GOOD (NOT JUST THE BAD AND THE UGLY)

Where Steven was dismissive, another client of mine, Lana, was delicate. Both struggled with curiosity, but it manifested in different ways in their lives.

Lana had just been hired as the youngest director on record for a large national nonprofit organization. Her position said, *I'm a high-powered executive who makes tough decisions and is comfortable in my own skin.* But inside, she struggled with a huge case of impostor syndrome, and she took criticism way too personally. If her boss wanted her to redo something, she felt like a terrible employee. If a coworker gave her side-eye during an important meeting, she assumed she was a horrible colleague. If her dog whined when she left the house, she was obviously an awful dog-mom. On the other hand, when people complimented her and gave her positive feedback, she found a way to invalidate their praise every time. Because criticism felt so shattering and compliments rang false, she fought input so fiercely that people became wary of communicating with her at all.

What Lana was missing was the self-confidence to listen to feedback with a curious, open mind. Without self-confidence, you will be defensive against both criticism and praise. When I say you should learn to take it *all* in, good and bad, I mean it. When it comes to the bad, you should listen when people try to teach you about yourself, but it's also okay if someone doesn't like you (most people don't even like themselves). Work on your self-confidence successfully, and you'll be amazed at how much less affected you are when other people try to convince you otherwise. When it comes to the good, it takes real emotional fitness to accept a compliment. This can be even tougher for some than sitting with criticism.

Lana had a lot of trouble with this. Whenever she received a compliment ("Great presentation today!"), she would cheat herself out of it by denying it ("No, no, I made a bunch of mistakes"), minimizing it ("Eh, it wasn't that great; I threw it together this morning"), or throwing another compliment right back ("It wasn't as good as your presentation yesterday!"). Together, we worked on taking this feedback in. One slow breath at a time, Lana practiced actually accepting compliments. She worked on allowing herself to feel them and express gratitude rather than protest. She even summoned the courage to ask for more information about what she did well ("Thank you so much! What part of the presentation resonated with you the most?"). Accepting both the good and the bad fuels personal growth.

If you're like me, you can probably easily remember someone being critical of you years ago, but it's tough to remember the times people have said nice things about you. One way to build up self-confidence over time is to create a "self-esteem file." Whether you use a physical notebook, your phone's notes app, or a file on your computer, create a space and fill it with every positive piece of feedback you've ever received. Maybe it's a customer who wrote a five-star review about your product, a colleague who was thankful that you championed their idea in a brainstorming session, or a family member who considers you their rock.

Any time a new piece of positive feedback comes to you, add it to the file. It may sound trite, but believe me, it boosts self-confidence. I have been keeping a self-esteem file for ten years. When I feel down or need a quick jolt of self-esteem, I look through all those years of feedback, and it's very compelling to read a decade's worth of data that shows that I have made a difference in people's lives. I immediately feel the clouds roll away in my head. Since we as humans tend to ruminate on negative feedback and forget the good—what we psychologists call the negativity bias—this exercise will keep you in touch with the positive reality of your effect on others.

CURIOSITY ABOUT OTHERS

One person who didn't lack curiosity was chef, writer, voyeur TV host, and self-proclaimed "enthusiast" Anthony Bourdain. Before his devastating suicide in 2018, Bourdain's raison d'être was his boundless curiosity. I loved his books and shows, particularly *Parts Unknown*: in every episode, he revealed a rich and delicious world wherever his frequent-flier miles could take him, and he would teleport his audience, too, luring them in with his infectious lust for rich cultural experiences. "Travel is about the gorgeous feeling of teetering in the unknown," he proclaimed. It wasn't just about the pursuit of food—he was in pursuit of connection and camaraderie in a diverse and complicated mix of humanity. And he wanted us to understand it, too. His arm was emblazoned with a tattoo that read in ancient Greek, "I am certain of nothing." Curiosity is a recognition of that sentiment.

As you get more comfortable being curious about yourself, you'll likely find yourself being more curious with others. Whether you have an important work interview, a first date, or a long weekend with your family, asking good questions will level up your experience immediately. Also, in purely selfish terms, asking people questions about themselves makes them like you more. According to researchers at Harvard, the number of questions you ask in a conversation correlates directly with the satisfaction experienced by the other person. People who ask nine or more questions in an exchange are found to be far more likable than those who ask fewer than four. Successful salespeople ask ten or more. That's why they're successful.

Conversation 101: How to Gain Curiosity

Now that you have a sense of how curiosity can help you grow, you may be thinking, *Okay, so how do I best build up this muscle?* The first step is to start with what Zen Buddhists call shoshin, or the beginner's mind: "In the beginner's mind, there are many possibilities, but in the expert's, there are few," Zen monk Shunryu Suzuki wrote in his book *Zen Mind, Beginner's Mind*. In other words, look at every situation you're placed in as if it's the first time you are in it. Or think about how children go into any new experience—they are naturally free of prejudice, preconceptions, or assumptions because they simply haven't lived enough life to get jaded and hardened.

Next, shore up those mindfulness muscles. When you're curiosity-deficient, you're likely to avoid potentially difficult conversations. *If I avoid this uncomfortable conversation*, the inner voice goes, *then I won't have to experience the uncomfortable feeling*. In truth, you can feel the discomfort now or deal with it tenfold later. The latter does not make for a winning long-term strategy. By embracing beginner's mind and leaning toward discomfort, you'll prepare yourself for the following three steps: listen, question everything, and take in what you hear.

LISTEN

The ability to participate in the balanced give-and-take of a conversation is a rare skill that too many people mistakenly believe they possess. Consider your conversational capacity for a moment. Do you listen, or simply wait until the other person is done speaking to shift things back to yourself, nodding along even as you're planning what you'll say? Be honest: Do you give your conversation partners time to pause and continue talking before jumping in with your thoughts?

Like running, listening with curiosity is hard to do but easy to train. All you need to run is a pair of sneakers. All you need for a good conversation is another person *and a willingness to listen*. Every day this week, start one conversation with a friend, peer, or partner with the express purpose of listening to what they have to say as deliberately as possible.

The first rule of listening is to do so *quietly*. Show you're present with nods, not words. Listening is a practice of getting comfortable with silence. When it comes to a difficult conversation, the first thing a person says generally isn't what they need you to know. Prompting them to go deeper by giving them some time to think shows them that you're present, interested, and ready to hear more. This will make them feel safe to open up. You'll be amazed at what people share when they're given that little bit of extra space. Silence is the most powerful conversation tool I know. Even when clients share a story they've told me before, I don't stop them. Instead, I assume that I didn't hear what they needed me to the last time, and I try to listen more deeply and with new ears, tuning in to clues I hadn't picked up on before. When in doubt, just listen.

QUESTION EVERYTHING

Think about the last time someone pointed out a mistake you made. What was your first instinct? To deny it? Make excuses? Apologize and try to move on quickly? If you react strongly to something someone says in your daily conversation, it's stirring up something important within you. Seek to understand that reaction. When discomfort arises, lean into the uncomfortable area with questions instead of pulling back defensively. Questions are the best alternative to defenses—they distract you from the discomfort of vulnerability while leading to greater insights.

One client of mine, Emma, often told stories that went nowhere. She never offered enough detail or context to allow me to make sense of the narrative. This made it incredibly difficult to help her process whatever her stories were intended to reveal. One day, Emma admitted to a pet peeve: she bristled at vague feedback from colleagues.

"I feel like they're saying quite a lot without saying anything at all," she complained to me one day.

Seeing the opening, I (gently) pointed out that I sometimes felt that way in our conversations.

Where many people might have reacted to this feedback defensively, Emma got curious—she asked me to explain more. She asked me for examples. She asked me if it was frustrating. I answered her questions, and we talked about where else this might be showing up in her life. She wondered if perhaps her frustration with her colleagues' vague feedback might be due, in part, to her own nebulous communication style. Thanks to her curiosity, Emma was able to hear my experience of her, think about it, and eventually, change it.

When someone comes to you with difficult feedback, dig down to get to the sometimes uncomfortable but deeply important stuff hiding beneath the surface. Instead of dismissing criticism, excusing your bad behavior, or refusing to share the blame, ask questions so you can correct course: "Can you say more about that?" does the trick. You might also ask, "Can you share some examples?" "How did you feel about that?" "What's that been like for you?" "How can I support you?" "What else do I need to know?" and "What could I do differently next time?" The only way to know is to ask.

TAKE IN WHAT YOU HEAR

Once you've listened and asked questions, the way you respond to what people tell you about yourself will (a) help you grow, and (b) inform what they share with you in the future. Here's how to take in constructive feedback to flex that curiosity muscle and get the best outcome.

1. Mirror back what you think the other person is trying to say. The goal is to ensure you're taking in what's being offered to you: "I think what I'm hearing is . . ." Listening is my job, yet I'm amazed by how often I reflect back to a client what I think I'm hearing and discover I've gotten it wrong.

2. Give yourself space between hearing the feedback and responding. When you respond right away, it can often be from a defensive place. To give yourself a few minutes to think, you might say, "I'd like a few minutes to think about that, and then we can talk about it."

3. Spend those minutes taking stock of your feelings. Do you feel defensive? Why is that? Do you feel misunderstood? Or is it something else? Take a few breaths to center yourself and remember that this critique is not about you as a person but just one facet of your behavior.

4. Thank the person for sharing. It's very vulnerable to give feedback, so acknowledge that. This is *not* the time to give feedback of your own, even if you think they're guilty of the same behavior.

5. Get curious. Ask questions to understand what effect your behavior has had on others. You can ask questions like: "Can you tell me more about that?" "How did it make you feel?" Or "What might I do differently next time?"

6. Let the person know that you're going to reflect on what's been said—and then make time to do that! To prioritize

growth, you have to build a muscle for taking in criticism as well as responding to it.

The Curiosity Push-Up: Solicit Feedback

When was the last time you explicitly asked someone for feedback? You might think of feedback as something you receive (sometimes against your will) in a work context. And yes, critical evaluation of your work performance and product will help you improve there. But feedback is also an extremely helpful tool in every part of your life as you work on your emotional fitness—specifically, it's a central part of your curiosity practice. We'll talk more about the importance of soliciting feedback in the next chapter, but this push-up will give you a chance to practice everything you've learned about curiosity.

> STEP 1: Take out your phone or computer and pull up a blank text or email. Get it ready to send to someone in your life whose perspective you respect. This could be a manager, colleague, report, spouse, friend, sibling, or child. In your message, **invite them to share one thing you're doing well and one thing you could do 10 percent better**. Here's a template you can use:
>
> *Hi! I'm working on my emotional fitness and today's challenge is to ask for feedback from someone whose perspective I value. And that's you! Would you be willing to share one thing I'm doing well as a friend / colleague / partner, and one thing I could do 10 percent better? Thank you for helping me become my best self.*

The last time I sent out this message (to a friend I see often), I received this back from her: "Wow I love this request! One thing you're doing well is that you're such a great communicator. I know I can trust you to tell me what you need and how you feel in our friendship—and you've taught me a lot about how to communicate as well. One thing you could do 10 percent better is to reach out to me proactively to hang out. Sometimes I feel like I'm always reaching out to you, and it makes me wonder if you value our friendship as much as I do!"

STEP 2: Once you receive a response, pay attention to your immediate reaction to their feedback. Do you feel defensive? Where do you feel it in your body? Was your knee-jerk reaction to disprove what they said or think of examples where it isn't true? Which aspect of their feedback created more discomfort for you—the negative or the positive?

My friend saying that I should initiate plans more surprised me, and at first, was hard to see. But after my initial reaction, I realized she had a point—I'm not always great at reaching out to people, even those I love the most. You don't have to accept everything you've heard. However, you *must* reckon with the way listening to it made you feel and what that might mean about you. Really consider this feedback, think about what it might offer to you. It can be tough to take these things in, but a wound must be open if you want it to heal.

STEP 3: Take action based on this feedback if necessary. Would incorporating this feedback, or acting on it, give you something valuable? If so, what is one concrete change you can make in your behavior as a result? After I received feedback from my friend, I set an alarm on my phone to remind me each month to reach out to her and to other friends who are important to me.

As you work your way through this exercise, do your best to take it all in and sit with it peacefully. As you receive responses, thank them for the gift. Because feedback is a gift. I recommend repeating this exercise at least once a month with different people in your life. I know this might feel awkward at first—maybe even every time you do it, but I promise it will be deeply helpful.

If you're feeling the burn by this point in your training, that's understandable. Training curiosity can be truly difficult, especially if you, like Steven, haven't made much use of it in the past. The payoff of lowering your defenses is that now you get to peek behind them, and behind those defenses lives incredibly important information about who you are. Now that you've flexed your curiosity muscles, you're ready to see what that information is. Let's jump into the next chapter, where you'll strengthen that very muscle: **self-awareness**.

5
SELF-AWARENESS
Knowing Thyself

We do not see things as they are, we see them as we are.

—ANAÏS NIN

Valerie, a young mother of two and HR manager at a midsize gaming company, seemed to have it all together. She had a great job, a loving relationship, and a wonderful community of friends. But as I looked closer, the cracks in her seemingly perfect facade showed. Valerie had come to see me because she just couldn't shake certain behaviors—behaviors she *knew* were counterproductive to her success and happiness at work. She was whip-smart and cared deeply about her job . . . so why couldn't she get her act together?

Despite her best efforts, Valerie found herself constantly procrastinating on important tasks, forgetting to finish assignments she'd promised to deliver, and letting her to-do list get completely out of control. She knew she needed to focus and get things done, but the more she tried to concentrate, the more she struggled. More problematic than her behavior, though, was the way she *felt* about her behavior. When she put something off until the last minute, even if she got it done in time, she grew deeply frustrated and angry with herself for it. The shame cycle was becoming overwhelming. Valerie didn't just worry that she was no good at her job. She started to fear she was no good as a person. In our first session, I asked her to share how she talks to herself when things go wrong. She confessed, "My inner voice is insanely harsh. When I mess up or fall short of perfection in any way, it's a continuous loop in my head, *What's wrong with you? You should have been able to do this. See, you aren't good enough, and you never will be.*"

Over time, I learned more about Valerie's behaviors—that she'd always had trouble focusing on boring tasks but could hyperfocus on interesting ones, that she constantly left drawers and cabinet doors open at home without realizing it (which drove her husband crazy), and that her stimulation-seeking behaviors distracted her. "My mind wanders to *anything* other than the task at hand—whether it's getting a snack from the kitchen, organizing my closet by color, or just scrolling on Instagram, I'm super distracted by any shiny object. Then, all of a sudden, hours have gone by, and the project I should have been doing is still sitting unfinished on my desk. On the other hand, when I do find something interesting or when a deadline is approaching, I'm a machine. It's like I can bend time and get absurd amounts of work done."

As I learned more about how Valerie thinks and works, one big revelation began to surface. "Valerie, with everything we've talked about in here, and how you seem to operate at home and in the office, I'm curious if you've ever explored the possibility that you might have ADHD." She looked at me, puzzled. I went on to explain a bit about what ADHD can look like and shared that while it would mean that her brain worked differently than other people's, it would not mean she couldn't be successful. ADHD can be harnessed as a superpower, but it can make productivity and success feel impossible when left unchecked. So many of the behaviors Valerie chastised herself for are typical of people with ADHD. But without knowing that, Valerie had chalked it all up to her being "broken" as a person.

I have ADHD myself—and, in fact, I conducted my doctoral research on it—so I knew a few things to be true. My research showed that for many people with ADHD, the shame of being told your whole life that there's something wrong with you is often more harmful than the ADHD symptoms themselves. It also showed that ADHD is not a life sentence to failure and disappointment. There is hope. Those who are given support to work *with* their ADHD instead of against it are much more likely to be successful. This support might look like picking the right type of work, receiving behavioral interventions or therapy, or even taking medication, but often it's as simple as believing that you are capable of learning and worthy of being taught.

Of course, before you can access any of the help that's out there for ADHD, you first have to know you have it. When I shared my suspicion with Valerie, she sat back in her chair, shocked. I knew she'd need some time to understand this information about herself, and I referred her for a formal assessment. Two weeks later, she showed up armed with articles about ADHD that she found online.

"Holy shit, Dr. E, I feel like someone just wrote about my entire life experience. This makes so much sense." Valerie expressed feeling like a bubble had popped in her life. "Realizing that all of my struggles are typical of ADHD has given me so much compassion for myself. Like maybe I'm *not* bad at everything. Maybe I just have a brain that works differently. I feel like I'm looking at things in a completely new way." It was a huge aha moment—but more revealing moments were to come.

Over time, Valerie and I started to understand that her harsh inner voice was the voice of her parents, two tough-as-nails military veterans who were always telling her that she should be doing better than she was. Her shelf of sports trophies and straight-A report cards weren't enough to get their praise. And whenever she did struggle—likely in part because of her undiagnosed ADHD— instead of trying to figure out the cause or seek help, her parents only deepened the wounds with questions like "What's wrong with you?" or "Why aren't you able to do this?" (Yes, the same bullying questions her inner voice used as an adult.)

Working with Valerie was rewarding because everything we discovered together felt like another key she could use to unlock her self-awareness and growth. Once she had a sense of *why* she spoke to herself so harshly—she had internalized and echoed that critical feedback she'd heard so much as a child—she realized she had two choices: she could let it continue or she could practice changing it. She decided that she wanted to treat herself with a bit more understanding and kindness. Instead of beating herself up when she made a mistake, she practiced speaking to herself the way she would to her daughter. *Hey, I know this is hard. That's because your brain works differently. What can you try here? What new strategies do you have? What kind of help can you ask for?*

Valerie's work to understand herself better had a huge ripple effect in all other aspects of her life. As she started to treat herself with more respect and compassion, it became easier to acknowledge her struggles and work through difficult moments. She learned to ask for accommodations at work—she asked her director to set clear project deadlines for her, she got a standup desk so she could move her body while working, and she brought on a virtual assistant to help with some of her tasks. She also joined a community of HR professionals with ADHD (yes, such groups exist!), and she prioritized her physical health because studies have shown that exercise is an important habit for those with ADHD. As her confidence in herself grew, her bosses noticed. Valerie was promoted twice in the two years we worked together.

Who Do You Think You Are?

Now that you've become a little more comfortable being uncomfortable and a bit more curious about yourself, here's an uncomfortable truth for you: it is an undeniable fact that we are notoriously bad at knowing ourselves. Our third trait, self-awareness, is the ability to understand your personality traits, triggers, biases, strengths, struggles, tendencies, and characteristics. It is a capacity to understand the role you are playing in your own relationships and your own life. While most people *believe* they are self-aware, research shows that only 10 to 15 percent of people actually demonstrate it. So much of who we *think* we are is based on assumptions, many of which are wrong. We can only view the world through the lens of our own experience, and if that lens is clouded, the consequences range from lost relationships to lost careers.

While self-awareness is one of the hardest of the seven traits to cultivate, it's too foundational to tackle last; otherwise, you will struggle with every other area. After all, it's pretty tough to change something about yourself before you know it exists. Learning to trace what you're feeling from moment to moment will help you respond appropriately instead of instinctively, taking full responsibility for yourself and your actions.

The whole concept of self-awareness is a tricky one: the more you know, the more you'll realize you *don't* know. There's always more to understand about yourself, and it should be considered a lifelong quest. Don't feel daunted, though—like with any exercise, the more you flex the muscle of self-awareness, the stronger it'll become. And now that you've learned to let down your defenses and get curious, you're in a position to see what's behind those defenses and get to know yourself in a deeper and more honest way.

Valerie's metamorphosis was made possible by getting to know herself in a new way and seeing things that she had hidden from herself or that hadn't been shown to her before. I know some might say that it should have been obvious that she had ADHD (I can't open social media these days without seeing a "Top Ten Signs You Have ADHD" post). But it's one thing to read a list of traits; it's another thing to have the perception and self-awareness to recognize those traits in yourself. Until we created the space together to allow her to spot the larger patterns in her behavior and connect the dots to a possible cause, she had been flailing. So much about self-awareness is exactly that: making room in your head and your heart to see what you couldn't see before. And what may be obvious to others may not be to you.

I've learned this lesson myself countless times. One such example: for years, I felt really frustrated with friends who spent all of our time together talking *at* me. They would fill hours telling me every detail of what was going on in their lives and never ask me any questions. I listened patiently, and from the outside, I did my best to stay present with what they were telling me. But on the inside, I burned. I kept quiet, though, no matter how much I wanted to scream, "You've been telling me about your day for an hour! What about my day? Don't you care about that?" I wanted to be a good friend, but inevitably, I would leave our hangouts feeling frustrated and resentful, and I wondered why I kept ending up with friends who took up so much space. It really felt like a "them problem."

What I didn't realize at the time was how much *I* was contributing to this dynamic. I have a big personality, and in group settings I love to talk and have the spotlight on me. But because of the work I do as a therapist, in one-on-one settings, I'm more comfortable being in a listening position. Maybe *too* comfortable. When I'm with my clients, my role is to center their needs and perspectives in our conversation. Was I unintentionally re-creating that dynamic in my friendships outside the office?

I realized that, in my interactions with friends, I was unconsciously diminishing myself and my ideas. When they asked me how I was doing, I would shift the focus back to them immediately. "I'm doing great, but how about you?" I wouldn't take the opportunity to talk about myself at all. Then, I'd sit seething as they spent the rest of the conversation talking about themselves—exactly as I'd prompted them to. Absurd, but there you have it.

Shawna, a close friend from college, finally pointed out this dynamic to me. Unlike many people, Shawna had the ability to strike a perfect balance between listening and talking. When Shawna asked me how I was doing and I said, "Great, but how about you?" she pushed back.

"Wait . . . we've barely talked about you, why are you asking about me already? Do you really want to just sit there and hear about my life without sharing anything about yours?"

Once I saw that I was *teaching* people to focus on themselves instead of on me, it felt less like a personal affront—and I realized I could change it. From then on, when friends asked how I was doing, I practiced sharing openly and tried to take up my fair share of the space. I even told some of them not to let me shift the focus back to them too quickly. I stepped in, my friends stepped up, and the dynamic changed drastically.

Renowned psychologist Carl Jung believed that until you make the unconscious conscious, it will rule your life, and you will call it fate. So many people feel like life is happening *to* them. They think

How Self-Aware Are You?

It can be tricky to assess your own self-awareness, because if you knew what you didn't know . . . well, you'd know it! But let's start with an exercise to see how it feels to reflect on yourself and your experiences. Sit down with your computer or a paper and pen and write out your answers to the following questions:

1. **What are your biggest strengths and superpowers?** For example, are you a great listener? A strategic thinker? Excellent at staying calm under pressure? How have you harnessed these strengths in your life? And how does the work you do leverage these strengths? How could you lean into these strengths even more?

2. **What are your biggest personal struggles that need your attention?** For example, do you tend to be impatient? Do you need to work on having better boundaries? Do you have trouble empathizing with people? How have these struggles kept you from achieving what you want at work and at home, and what is standing in the way of you working through them?

3. **What motivates you and gives you a sense of purpose?** What are your values? For example, do you most value integrity? Success? Community? Learning? How do you see your values play out in your work and personal life? Do the choices you make align with these values? If not, why might that be? (To get a better sense of your values, google *value sort exercise* and try one of the free options.)

4. Now turn it around: **How do you think your friends, family, and coworkers see you?** Would they use the same words to describe you as you use to describe yourself? Do they share feedback with

you about how you're doing as a friend, family member, or colleague? If not, why might that be?

Next, reflect on how it felt to answer these questions. Was it
difficult? Interesting? Uncomfortable? If you had trouble answering, you likely have some work to do. If you answered them confidently, you're off to a great start! But it's likely that some of your
answers are incomplete—self-awareness is a moving target and
an ongoing practice.

they have no agency and have to endure whatever is thrown their
way. With self-awareness, you will come to realize that you are creating your reality in so many ways. And once you realize it, you can
change it. That is what we are trying to do in this chapter—to make
what has been largely unconscious conscious. Have you been walking through life without enough self-awareness? Well, let's find out.

Holding Up the Mirror

Self-awareness is powerful. When you're self-aware, you will make
better decisions. You will be more patient, understanding, and resilient, so you can handle frustrating moments and better manage
your emotions. You will have a larger reservoir of willpower and
determination to achieve your most important goals. You will be a
more confident, successful, well-rounded leader and show up better
for your colleagues and coworkers, and at home, you will be more
present for the people you love.

Sounds like a great place to be, right? But, of course, it's easier
said than done. To build self-awareness, you first have to come to

terms with a very primal instinct in yourself, and that is self-preservation. While human beings are highly intelligent creatures with complex minds, we are also wired to do one thing: survive. One way you do that is to *avoid* your pain so you can continue to function, and sometimes, the most painful thing you can face is your own demons. *Nothing to see here*, you might think, and you will always be on guard to protect that assumption. You might see yourself one way and act another, never realizing that your ideas about yourself and your behavior are in conflict.

To illustrate this, I often pull out this exercise in my talks: I'll ask everyone to turn to the person next to them; one person is to make a fist with their hand (I usually randomly ask for the person with the shorter hair to do it). I then tell the other person that they have five seconds to get their partner's fist open.

"On your mark, get set, go . . ."

Chuckles fill the room as I watch one half of participants try to pry their partner's clenched fist open as the other half battles to keep their fist as tightly closed as they possibly can.

When time is up, I check in with the people who made the fist.

"Those of you who were making a fist—how many of you resisted your partner opening it?"

The majority of fist-makers' hands go up.

"So, my question for you is . . . why? I never provided that instruction, I never told you to make this exercise as difficult as possible for your partner."

I then speak to those who tried to get their partner's fist open.

"To those who were directed to open the fist, how many of you tried to pry your partner's fist open like the Jaws of Life?"

Same response. Most of the fist "priers" giggle and raise their hands.

I respond, "So I have a question for you. Why didn't you just say,

'Hey, we're doing this activity together, I'm supposed to get your fist open, would you mind going ahead and opening it for me?'"

People tend to laugh at this point, but I can practically hear the cogs and wheels churning in their heads as I help them see something about themselves that they probably wouldn't have identified. I explain that their instinct to keep their fist clenched closed or to pry their partner's fist open comes from a very human tendency to default to a "me versus you" mindset, rather than a collaborative or "us versus the problem" mindset (more on this in later chapters). There was no reason to assume that this activity was adversarial, and most of the people in those rooms are kind people who likely identify as being very collaborative. But every human being is defensive sometimes, even when they don't really need to be.

This is why self-awareness and curiosity are so deeply linked—the less defensive you are, the more you'll learn about yourself, and the more you know about yourself, the more you'll understand places where you might get defensive. When you know where and why and with whom you tend to be defensive, you can decide whether or not you really need to protect yourself. If I had everyone do that same "make a fist" activity again, it would be unlikely that they would approach it as competitively. So, whenever you notice yourself in that "me versus you" mindset, whenever you feel nervous or competitive or judged—think of this "make a fist" exercise—you might see your reaction as an opportunity to learn more about yourself.

One of my clients, Keller, *really* hated being told what to do. Any implication, especially from his boss, that he should do something differently completely set him off. He told me that whenever his manager called him into her office, his chest would tighten.

"If she calls me out on a 'mistake,' I list off all the reasons why my ideas are valid and why I shouldn't be doubted. And it's not like she's being unfair or cutting—she's actually a pretty cool boss—but I boil with rage at the slightest criticism, and I end up raising my voice and making a scene."

"It sounds like you head into every conversation ready for a fight, which is probably not the best approach with the person who determines your salary."

"I know, *I know*. But I can't seem to help it."

In addition to exploring his resistance to authority (Keller's last boss micromanaged his every move, never leaving any room for him to try things or express himself), I worked with Keller to practice creating some space between himself and his actions. He learned to ask himself, *Why do I feel so tense right now? What am I worried about? Is this reaction warranted in this situation? What investment does this person have in helping me versus making my life harder?* Keller knew he was sensitive to being micromanaged, so before every one-on-one with his boss, he practiced taking three slow breaths before walking into her office. While he did this, he reminded himself that his manager is not against him and that ultimately they're on the same team. And as he started doing this, he noticed himself reacting much less defensively. That's the power of self-awareness. By acknowledging your emotions, you can change the very chemistry of them, alter your behavior, and flip your outcome from a conflict to a resolution.

Like Valerie, we all build walls, overlook information, and avoid triggers . . . and like my audience members and Keller, we all go on the defense sometimes without really knowing we're doing so. When self-awareness is weak, maladaptive patterns are often repeated, people act on biases without realizing it, and personal growth stagnates. But your attempts to protect yourself from painful truths might be keeping you from knowing important things about yourself. Let's take a look at how to strengthen this important muscle.

Achieving Self-Awareness

Self-awareness is a moving target, which means there's always more work to do. So how do you build this elusive trait of self-awareness? The following are three approaches that I recommend, and they build on one another: (1) introspection, where you'll practice looking inward and asking yourself tough questions; (2) therapy, where you'll get support acknowledging difficult truths; and finally, (3) feedback, where you'll expand on what you learned in the last chapter and get into the regular habit of inviting others to help you become more aware of yourself.

KEEP LOOKING INWARD: INTROSPECTION

To keep yourself physically healthy, you need to keep track of your vitals, which are go-to indicators of how your body is functioning: you step on a scale to check your weight, you get your cholesterol levels tested by a doctor, you check your heart rates while on the treadmill. The same is true with your self-awareness—you should regularly check in about where you are emotionally. One way you can do that is through a regular practice of introspection—asking yourself questions and answering them, thoughtfully and honestly. As simple as it sounds, sitting with your thoughts is hard to do. One 2014 comprehensive study published in *Science* magazine analyzed eleven studies that showed participants preferred doing mundane activities such as watching TV or reading a boring book over sitting with their thoughts for even six to fifteen minutes. Many even preferred to administer electric shocks to themselves rather than sit and think. They chose self-inflicted physical pain over looking inward! This is a great example of the lengths people will go to avoid their thoughts and feelings.

I'm here to tell you that with practice, self-reflection doesn't have to be quite so painful. You just need a little direction and support. You'll also need the mindfulness and curiosity we talked about in the previous two chapters—for a thought or feeling to be seen, you have to be open to seeing it. What does this look like? It can be as simple as a few minutes of deliberate reflection each day, as if you are holding up a mirror to yourself. The practice of self-inquiry is all about asking yourself questions. Everyone will have different questions to ask themselves, but to start, take any situation you're currently navigating, or any situation you had a tough time understanding in the past, and reflect on it.

Let's say you had an awkward conversation with your boss during a performance review. Maybe they gave you some tough feedback—"I need to see more from you in this next quarter"—and you found yourself being defensive. If you have enough awareness to know that the conversation could have gone better, then you're in a great spot. Set aside some time and break down why you think things went the way they did. And think about the triggers and biases that steer you. Here are some prompts to help you along.

- *What was I feeling when this happened and why?* Perhaps you felt angry? Hurt? Rejected? Sidelined? Underappreciated? The feelings you're comfortable with might be guarding the ones you're less comfortable with (for example, maybe you're comfortable being angry but uncomfortable being sad). Owning all of your emotions is an important first step so that you can make an intentional decision about how to communicate and/or act on them.

- *What meaning did I make of the other person's behavior?* The meaning we make of people's behavior tends to be filled with assumptions. Perhaps you assumed that your boss doesn't like you, and that's why they gave you that feedback. Can you try to see the situation from a different point of view? What else could be going on to explain things (for example, is it possible your boss believes in your potential and wants to hold you to a higher standard)?

- *How do I tend to react in situations like this one?* Perhaps when you feel criticized, you tend to fight back, apologize too quickly, or share all the reasons why people are wrong. By knowing and owning your patterns, you will be more likely to make different and better choices the next time. Think back to the last few instances where you've felt this way and see if there are any patterns to how you reacted.

You can use these prompts for any scenario to help you delve deeper into your thoughts, behaviors, and motivations. Remember that self-awareness is a continuous journey—it takes practice. Keep trying to better understand and empower yourself in making intentional and informed choices at work and at home.

It's important to keep an eye on your struggles, but you should also keep an eye on your strengths. Successful people are aware of the personality traits that helped them achieve their success. Remember: strengths without awareness become weaknesses, but strengths examined regularly become superpowers. Remember Steven from the previous chapter? The go-getter who believes in himself and can push past people who tell him no or "you're never going to succeed" will get further than someone who lets other people's doubts derail him. But this strength weakens as quickly as an overused muscle if he becomes so stubborn that he ignores valid feedback.

One of the best tools out there for any kind of introspection is journaling. Writing is an incredibly powerful tool for processing your emotions, so don't spare the ink. Your thoughts sound different spinning around in your head than they will when you look at them written down in front of you. Get into a regular journaling practice, even if you write just one line a day about how you felt that day. If you need help, many books offer great prompts for reflection, like the classic *The Artist's Way* by Julia Cameron, *The Mountain Is You* by Brianna Wiest, or Sharon Jones's *Burn After Writing* series. Over time, you'll see patterns emerge, you'll gain perspective on what you're feeling, and you'll have a record of your internal world to refer back to.

NAME YOUR FEELINGS

Benjamin and I started working together after his girlfriend broke up with him and his boss fired him the same month. Each week, he'd come in and look at me expectantly, waiting for me to tell him how to solve his problems. Instead, I checked in with him about his life that week and how he was feeling. The problem was that Benjamin had no idea how to talk about how he was feeling. He would either tell me thoughts disguised as feelings: "I feel like my boss should have been fired instead of me," or he would use the same few words to communicate how he felt: "I don't know . . . bad, I guess."

Over time I came to understand that Benjamin wasn't good at describing his feelings because growing up, he wasn't really encouraged to *have* feelings, and he certainly wasn't taught how to express them. We humans aren't born with the language to communicate what's happening inside of us—that's taught to us, ideally by our parents and caregivers. When a child cries because he was refused a toy, his parents have an opportunity to teach him how to put words to his feelings. They might say, "Are you feeling angry right now because I said no? It's frustrating when we don't get what we want." This is how a child learns to identify what anger feels like. The parent who ignores the tears, or berates or shames the child for crying, teaches the child that his feelings are invalid and should be pushed away.

Many people come up short in describing their feelings, but until you understand what you're experiencing, it can be tough to lean into your emotions, and tougher to ask for support. If you have a hard time articulating how you feel, there are graphs and charts online that can help (google *feelings wheel* for a great place to start). Try getting specific when expressing your emotions. So if you feel sad right now, are you lonely? Bored? Vulnerable? If you're happy, are you excited? Grateful? Proud? As you become more familiar with different feelings words, you'll get better at recognizing and talking about feelings, as well as specifying those hard-to-pinpoint emotions.

All this said, solo introspection only goes so far—there are many things about yourself that will be hard to access because of the default defenses laid out in the curiosity chapter. Sometimes you need the support of someone from the outside who can help hold up a mirror and connect dots that are hard for you to see.

COLLABORATIVE GROWTH: THERAPY

No world-class athlete would ever achieve their full potential without a coach . . . why would you expect to reach your emotional potential by yourself? Having a trained, objective person to reflect you back to yourself is invaluable. (Pro tip here—your friends and family are an important type of support, but they're not trained, and they're not objective.) Consider investing in someone who can help you see things you may not readily see. That's where a good therapist can come in.

Many people believe that to "deserve" therapy, they need to be in dire straits—in the throes of a divorce or job loss. Therapy still has a lot of stigmas around it. Many people delegate therapy to those who have "major problems," neglecting the fact that it can be wonderfully beneficial to all. Emotional fitness is hard to do alone, and therapy is for anyone who wants to better understand who they are in the world and to improve the relationships they have with themself and with other people. In therapy you'll do a deeper kind of work—you'll build muscles to avoid emotional struggles and get better prepared for when life throws you inevitable curveballs down the road.

I learned this myself when I went to my first therapy session in 2009, during my first year of grad school for clinical psychology. I didn't start therapy because I thought I needed it. I believed I was a well-adjusted and very self-aware person, thank you very much! But I wanted to sample the product I was training to sell, so I started with a therapist. I can't help but look back at myself and laugh at how much I didn't know I didn't know.

At first, it didn't feel like much was happening in therapy. I felt like I was doing a bit of role-playing—testing out what it would be like for my future clients. Of course, it was also nice to have a place to vent about my day. But a few months in, something I probably couldn't have predicted came up. Before therapy, I was the type of person who would tear up in any emotional situation; anytime I felt sad, angry, or overwhelmed, my eye ducts would fill up. This happened in important meetings and in serious conversations where I would really have preferred to keep my composure. I didn't like this about myself—it made me feel like I wasn't in control of my emotions. So when I first started therapy and I could feel the water works turning on, I'd tell my therapist, "Don't pay attention when I get teary. The fact that I'm crying doesn't mean anything. . . . This is just what happens to me."

She obliged, but the next time it happened (and the next and the next), she would gently point it out and patiently ask what I was feeling in that moment. In one session, I was telling her a story about a friend who let me down, and I began to tear up. I tried to rush past it and minimized both the tears and the way my friend had made me feel, but she stopped me and said, "Press pause, Emily. It's okay that tears are coming up. Let's listen to what they're trying to alert us to. Take a breath, and tell me what you're feeling right now."

When I did, it became clear—I was angry at my friend and sad that she let me down. But I didn't want to admit it to myself because then I'd have to do something about it. Acknowledging the feelings helped them pass, and I was able to think more clearly about how to handle the situation. Over time, and many more examined (instead of ignored) tears, my therapist helped me understand that these tears were a physical manifestation of all of the emotions I had never allowed myself to feel. They were pieces of information that I should pay attention to, not fight off. And when I finally started to give them some space to fall instead of pushing them away, I noticed myself tearing up less and less out in the world.

This was something that would have been tough to know about myself on my own. I needed a compassionate other to reflect something to me that I was working hard not to know about myself—that I had a whole host of emotions that wanted to be felt. This realization helped me see the power of therapy and the way it can deepen self-awareness. Through therapy, I learned so much about my patterns, uncovered buried emotions, and accepted that *I* am the common factor in all of my life circumstances.

Remember this, though: as helpful as therapy was, there was no one aha moment that changed my entire life. There's a misconception that therapy is only working when you have sudden bursts of clarity, but that's not the case most of the time. Progress tends to be gradual, and it takes a lot of hard work. It was that way for me: I was in therapy for many years, and then at some point, I looked around and noticed that everything in my life had shifted for the better. My relationships were healthier, I was being clearer with my needs and boundaries, I was more resilient when tough things happened to me—and yes, I was crying less in serious meetings. I saw firsthand—in and out of the "classroom"—how powerful it is to have a trained, objective person to help me sort through my emotions. And I became a better therapist because of it.

Of course, I recognize that therapy is expensive and time-consuming. There are very real barriers to getting into therapy—whether they're financial, geographical, or situational. Even today, not everyone has access to health insurance and even those who do may not have an insurance plan that covers mental health costs. And while the stigma around therapy has somewhat eased (but still has a way to go), this has created another problem: a shortage of therapists, which makes it harder to set up an appointment and get help when it's needed. Society has a *very* long way to go here, and I don't want to underplay how frustrating the process can be. At the same time, there are sliding-scale clinics in every major city that provide lower-cost therapy, and there are online options that are more cost-effective.

Remember, too: time shrinks and expands in relation to your priorities. I have so many friends who told me that they didn't think they had the time or money for therapy but that once they started, they couldn't imagine spending their time or money on anything more valuable. Can you imagine if an Olympic athlete ate fast food every day and said they were too busy to nourish their bodies with healthy food? How the hell are they going to win gold eating only burgers and fries? Your mind is your greatest asset for your success, and it's important to invest in it accordingly.

ASK AROUND: FEEDBACK

Once you've gotten more comfortable with introspection, inside or outside of therapy, it's imperative to check in with those who interact with you and know you from a different angle. In other words, it's time to solicit some feedback. You started this practice with your push-up in the previous chapter; keep it going by integrating it regularly into your everyday life. This is uncomfortable for many people, and I get it—no one wants to hear that they've let someone down (and many people have just as much trouble accepting compliments!). But feedback has enormous benefits for your growth. Sports coaches and players review highlight game reels as a learning tool—you need to review your past actions and behaviors in order to improve your future interactions.

Valerie and I worked on her reactions to feedback. She knew she avoided asking for it, and we figured out why: any criticism seemed to confirm her underlying fear that she wasn't good enough. For instance, after giving a presentation at work, Valerie didn't even look at the results from the feedback survey that was sent to everyone who attended. She didn't really want to know how people felt about it. A week later, she had to give the presentation again to her boss. Afterward, her boss took her aside and told her: "I could tell you worked so hard on your presentation, but the slides were a bit all over the place and unorganized. Did you look at the feedback you got the last time? Several people mentioned this. I'm confused as to why you didn't update it."

In Valerie's mind, her boss had told her that she was useless and the presentation was a failure. But really, I pointed out, he was reminding Valerie that she could have easily improved it had she read the feedback that was sent to her. As Valerie started to work on softening her harsh inner voice and her belief that she should always be doing better than she was, she became more comfortable taking in feedback, and eventually, she sought it out actively.

Many psychologists divvy up self-awareness into two camps: internal and external. Internal self-awareness is all about knowing who you are at your core—your passions and values, your triggers and your biases—while external self-awareness is about understanding how other people see you. Getting feedback from other people will help you with both internal and external awareness—as you learn how others see you, you can compare that to how you see yourself. If the two are largely different, it probably means you have some work to do.

Asking for feedback is not typically a natural, easy thing to do; it can conjure up a lot of doubts and insecurities, so people tend to shy away from it. This can be for all kinds of reasons: For one thing, many people don't have any model for what helpful feedback is supposed to look and feel like. You might avoid asking for constructive feedback because you're afraid of what you'll hear. You might avoid asking for positive feedback because you feel like it's not okay to fish for validation or praise. But soliciting feedback (both positive and negative) is a very powerful way to build self-awareness, and people often won't share their thoughts and feedback until you ask for it.

Feedback can also be tough at any career level: When you're just starting out, a boss won't hesitate to tell you where you need work.

A peer might chime in if the problem is truly glaring. As you move up the ladder, though, it becomes increasingly unlikely that the people around you will help you grow. A direct report will probably change jobs before confronting you with your flaws. A boss may just fire you rather than coach you into improvement. And personal growth stalls for many leaders because their success and power insulate them from useful feedback. The solution to this conundrum is to solicit feedback actively—at any life stage.

With effort and practice, you will strengthen your ability to stay open to life as you're living it. Feedback will no longer scare you. Instead, you'll seek it out from family, friends, and coworkers. Ultimately, you'll see that there is more than one way to be in the world and that some ways of being work better than others. With self-awareness, you'll have the freedom to choose for yourself.

The Self-Awareness Push-Up: Join, Jealous, or Jump?

It's time to drop and give me twenty. Remember the defense mechanism called projection? It's so much easier to see flaws in other people than it is to recognize them in yourself. Your emotional push-up for self-awareness is all about owning the role you might be playing in your frustrations with other people. I do this exercise every time I feel annoyed, angry, frustrated, or judgmental toward someone else.

> STEP 1: Think of the last time you felt judgmental of someone's behavior or temperament. Maybe you have a coworker who is a know-it-all, a boss who micromanages you, or a friend who never asks you any questions about how you're doing. My example: Years ago, in grad school, there was a

fellow student in my cohort who was excessively attention-seeking. He spoke over everyone, interrupted me in class, and hogged focus in every group setting. I noticed that his behavior seemed to bother me more than it bothered other people in my group, which told me that there was something there to learn about *myself.*

STEP 2: Ask yourself what *meaning* you're making of the behavior. In my example, my fellow students might have seen this attention hog and thought, *Wow, he's really passionate about this subject.* But the meaning I made of it was, *This guy thinks he's better than everyone and doesn't respect other people's opinions.* The meaning you make of a behavior is generally what you're reacting to, more than the behavior itself, so it's important to get clear on how you're interpreting things.

STEP 3: Examine the three J's. Any time you feel judgmental, annoyed, or frustrated with another person, there might be one of three reactions happening, which at Coa, we call Join, Jealous, and Jump. When I noticed myself feeling really annoyed with this fellow student, I checked in with myself about these three J's:

- **Join.** Am I aggravated with this person's behavior because I recognize this negative trait in myself? Is this a case of, as the saying goes, "If you spot it, you've got it"? In my situation with the attention-seeking student, I had to ask myself, *Am I also attention-seeking? Do I sometimes think my ideas are more important than other people's? And if so, is this something I don't really like about myself?*

- **Jealous.** Am I annoyed with this behavior because, deep down, I'm actually envious that this person has a resource, ability, or form of external recognition or support that I want for myself? I had to check in with myself, *Might I feel some envy that this student had such an easy time asking for attention? Maybe I wished I was a little better at that.*

- **Jump.** Did this behavior frustrate me because it brought up something unpleasant from my past? This step is called jump because you are jumping back to a past situation or relationship that brings up feelings in a current one. As a middle child, I didn't get all the attention I wished I had growing up, so I had to wonder, *Did I transpose that feeling about my siblings onto this student?*

Think through these three J's, and get really honest with yourself about which one (or two, or three) of them might be contributing to your frustration with this other person. And then, once you have an understanding about how you might be contributing to the dynamic, ask yourself how you want to act on it. In my situation, I realized some of my frustration with my fellow student came from the knowledge that I can be a bit attention-seeking, too. Once I let myself know this, I decided that rather than trying to chastise him for his behavior, I should probably start by working on my own.

If you do this self-awareness exercise consistently, you'll get better at noticing the ways your negative emotions are generated by your own issues and often only *triggered* by the behavior of others. The acknowledgment of this alone will help lessen the intensity of your emotions, which will make it easier to choose an appropriate response.

I ran through this exercise with Cara, for example, a data analyst who came to see me for help maintaining her sobriety as she stepped into a high-stress leadership role. Cara was feeling extremely frustrated with a boss who would sugarcoat criticism, withhold difficult information, and avoid giving direct feedback, even when Cara asked for it. "I think my boss is trying to protect my feelings, but I just see it as being dishonest, which makes it hard for me to trust or like him."

Cara and I ran through the three J's together. Join resonated immediately.

"Well, if I'm honest with myself, I've done a lot of sugarcoating and avoiding the truth in my day. Anywhere there's addiction, there are secrets, too. I know that honesty is the best policy, but sometimes I still act in similar ways to how my boss does. I can imagine some of my frustration with him might come from not loving that aspect of myself."

Jealousy didn't factor in with Cara's assessment—at first. But when she started to really think about it, she realized she *was* a bit envious—envious that her boss seemed to have risen through the ranks at the company without ruffling feathers or upsetting anyone with direct feedback. Everyone on the team really liked her boss, probably because he focused only on the positive, and it often fell to Cara to give out bad news.

Finally, how about jump? Cara reflected on the fact that, having parents who struggled with addiction as well, the game of deception was played nearly every day. Having family who never told her the truth, even when she could feel it, made her hyperaware of anyone not being direct with her. Cara realized that her frustration with her boss was at least partially leftover frustration from many years of feeling in the dark with her family.

Contextualizing her frustration helped Cara realize that she was taking her boss's behavior more personally than it was intended, and she decided to have a thoughtful conversation with him about it.

These three J's may not always resonate with you, but checking in with yourself every time you're frustrated with someone else is a great practice to build self-awareness. Regularly ask yourself what other people's behavior triggers in you. This isn't navel-gazing. It's about taking responsibility for your thoughts and making intentional choices about your behavior—because at the end of the day you can't control what other people do or feel, but you can control how you react. Acknowledging the role you play in your relationships will give you a lot of agency in them.

Every human being has trouble with this sometimes. Seeing how you may be responsible for your frustrations is uncomfortable. Taking in tough feedback can be downright painful. But you can handle it better than you think you can, and you can use what you learn to get through difficult moments and situations in your life. Ready to improve this ability? Let's get **resilient**.

6
RESILIENCE
Bouncing Forward

> *You wouldn't ask why the rose that grew from the concrete had damaged petals. On the contrary, we would all celebrate its tenacity. We would all love its will to reach the sun.*
>
> —TUPAC SHAKUR

Ari was a precocious and dedicated entrepreneur. Voted "Most Likely to Be the Next Mark Zuckerberg" in his high school yearbook, Ari had already started three companies by the time he turned eighteen. Right after graduating college (in three years), he started a new venture that helped companies build out their social media platforms. He loved it—he breathed, slept, and ate founder life, spending every moment thinking about ways to innovate, and he had built an impressive list of clients, from international retail stores to gaming sites. Ari invested every dollar to his name in this company, and he had friends and family who were financially and emotionally invested as well. It was a spectacular success, until it became a spectacular failure.

Ari's innovative approach had created a problem: he was so good at getting results that his clients quickly maximized their profits beyond expectations, and they didn't need him anymore after the initial push. He needed to add another vertical that kept clients coming back for more. Ari explored every avenue he could think of, from developing a proprietary analytics tool to offering personalized social media strategy consultations. The analytics tool, while promising, required more resources than the company could allocate at the time. The consultation service, although well received, didn't provide the recurring revenue stream that was desperately needed. Ari found himself caught in a loop of trial and error, learning valuable lessons with each iteration but struggling to find the elusive solution that would propel his venture back into success. Despite his tireless efforts, the harsh reality of the start-up world began to set in—the path to success is often paved with failures, and even the most well-intentioned ideas can fall short in execution. Ari's once-thriving start-up was on the brink of collapse.

And it wasn't just his work life that wasn't working—right around this time, his long-term relationship ended, he had to move out of his apartment, and his beloved dog passed away. Discouraged by the lack of progress at work and overwhelmed with his life events, Ari reverted to the company's original model and watched in resignation as profits stagnated and then plummeted. To cut bait with the banks, he had to shutter the business without much notice. Employees were upset with him. Clients were upset with him. He was full of anxiety and shame, and because he took his stress out on family and close friends, his normally strong support structure was feeling precarious. Ari described this time as the lowest in his life.

Many who have gone through such an ordeal may think, *I should take a step back and think about my next move.* Not Ari. He immediately threw himself into raising capital for another company without processing the loss of his previous venture. To ensure a different outcome, however, he came to me for some guidance. What became clear to me very quickly—and I see it a lot—was that he had not taken the time to understand how traumatizing the last situation had been before he pushed on to the next stressful thing. And it was clearly affecting how he showed up at his new company. He based decisions rashly and singularly on trying to avoid prior mistakes while being shortsighted in the longer term. When people asked him how he was doing, he would say "Everything's great," while forcing a smile. Ari was overwhelmed and unhappy, but he rammed right on through.

Some people might see Ari as resilient—he didn't let his failed company get him down; he went right on to the next thing with a smile on his face, so he must be doing great, right? But what I saw when I sat with Ari was the exact opposite: he wasn't being resilient . . . he was setting himself up for failure. When I asked him how he felt about having to shut down his company, he said, "It is what it is. I'm totally fine. And even if I wasn't, I don't have time to worry about it." But he was drinking every night of the week, his nails were bitten down to nubs, and he couldn't remember the last time he'd gotten a good night's sleep. Ari was avoiding his pain and doing everything he could to resist the negative feelings that he was experiencing, and I knew this would catch up to him in a devastating way if he didn't change course.

"Do you realize that what you went through with your last company is similar to a death?" I asked Ari one day, hoping he might see the way he was minimizing all he'd been through. "It doesn't sound like you gave yourself much time to grieve."

"Grieve? I don't really think about it that way. It felt like the best thing I could do was put my head down and keep going. Like, what would wallowing do for me? In the entrepreneurial world, you're only as good as your last IPO, and I didn't want people to forget about me, or worry that I had lost my touch. That burden seemed bigger than how I was feeling about it all."

"I definitely understand that, but just like I wouldn't expect you to shove down your feelings and push forward right after a death in your family, I don't want you to cheat yourself out of the important opportunity to grieve the loss of this company that you put so much of your time, energy, resources, and identity into. Your company's failure doesn't make *you* a failure; even with all the best planning, some things simply don't work out. But before you get back in the ring, you need to process it all, learn from the experience, and use what you gained to your advantage."

I wasn't sure if he was ready to let himself feel everything he'd pushed away for so long, but he looked relieved, took a deep breath, and told me he was open to turning toward his grief instead of away from it.

There is a huge misconception about grief—that it's only for the loss of loved ones, but really, grieving should take place anytime anything important to you is lost. Divorce, a job, an illness, even a missed opportunity, like failing to get a promotion, or, in Ari's case, losing a big business venture and all the dreams he attached to it. And grief can look like a lot of things—sometimes, it follows the classic path laid out by Dr. Elisabeth Kübler-Ross in her stages of grief: denial, anger, bargaining, depression, and, finally, acceptance. But more often than not, it's an unpredictable process that asks you to acknowledge what you've been through, let yourself feel it, and get the support you need to move forward. As frustrating as it can be, it's a process that needs time to work in order for you to heal. Not grieving is like returning to the gym too quickly after an injury. You risk reinjury—making the problem ten times worse. You have to pause. Regroup. Reset. The way I saw it, Ari was at risk of reinjuring himself emotionally. And until he understood that the only way out is through, he would set himself up to fail again.

Life Is a Stress Test

I define resilience as the ability to bounce forward through setbacks and failures. Notice that I use the phrase bounce *forward* instead of bounce back, because like it or not, you'll never go back to being the person you were before you went through a hard thing, and that shouldn't be your goal. Resilience is the ability to acknowledge whatever challenge you're facing, reflect on it, learn from it, and use it as a springboard to grow into a better version of yourself. Resilience isn't about pretending things are fine when they're not. It isn't about smiling through struggle. Resilient people don't let failure stop them; they push forward, but they do so *thoughtfully*, with their eyes wide open, and with an honest perspective about how they feel and what they need. Maintaining a positive attitude is all well and good, but if you do so in lieu of working through your pain, it only adds to the struggle.

Resilience is a hugely important trait to cultivate because it is absolutely inevitable that you will face many challenges in your life—big, small, and everything in between. Life involves pain. I'm here to tell you that there's just no way around that, and the sooner you can accept it, the sooner you can deal with it. If you've already faced a lot of adversity in your life, you might do everything in your power to avoid it. Or, you might even feel comfortable in a place of struggle because it's what you've known. Those who have faced less adversity might not have confidence in their ability to face and move through difficult moments. Every single day in my office I see people try to shortcut their struggles. They ignore them, avoid them, and numb them. And if that worked, I'd be the first to support it. But it doesn't. Instead, you need to hone your ability to face your challenges head-on, and find and make use of resources that keep you moving toward all you want to accomplish and become in life.

When I was researching the seven traits, a lot of words came up to describe getting through tough times—*commitment, grit, perseverance*, and *resolve*, to name just a few. But the one that seemed to encompass everything was *resilience*. And despite what some people may believe, the true key to this trait is not strength. It's adaptability. In nature, Charles Darwin talked about survival of the fittest, but he was really speaking about survival of the most adaptable. Birds fly south for the winter to find food. Chameleons change color to avoid predators. Animals, insects, and plants of all kinds do what they need to do to survive.

Humans are no different. The most successful are those who can adapt to a changing environment. And while some people are born with more natural resilience than others, and many people were forced to be resilient far earlier than they should have been, resilience is a skill that can be learned, practiced, and strengthened. I can't shield you from the painful things that will happen to you— that's life—but I can show you how to handle them better.

Life is a continuous stress test, whether it's the twists and turns of climbing the career ladder or facing things far beyond your control, like a global pandemic. The way you face and move through these moments will define your success. The work you've done and are doing on mindfulness, curiosity, and self-awareness will help you build your resilience. Now that you've practiced tolerating your discomfort, recognizing your struggles, and leaning into your strengths, a new type of hard work begins.

From Avoidant to Stuck

While Ari was avoiding his emotions, Caitlyn was stuck in hers. Caitlyn was a recent graduate who had landed a coveted entry-level job at a big streaming company. She loved being in the creative media environment and all the exciting perks that go with it, like going to movie premieres and working with famous directors. And she was good at it, too: She was smart, a fast learner, and a dedicated team player. When a higher-up left, she saw a big opportunity to move up. She'd done all the right things: she boldly put herself up for the promotion, gathered evidence of all her hard work, and wrote a stellar letter about how she was the right fit for the role. She knew she could do the job—she had the performance reviews to prove it, after all.

Unfortunately, she didn't get it. When she asked why, her boss told her that she simply wasn't ready. Caitlyn was devastated. And angry. Really angry. So angry that she let it consume her, and it started to affect her work. She missed deadlines, showed up late to the office, and appeared unengaged in meetings. Her boss noticed. When he called her out about it, Caitlyn thought to herself, *Well, if you actually recognized my hard work, maybe I'd show up on time.* Caitlyn talked about how she'd been wronged to everyone who would listen. And even as her support network validated her disappointment and reminded her that she would have more opportunities, Caitlyn fell deeper into a pit of anger and despair. She was so stuck in her disappointment that she could not move forward and, in fact, was making things worse for herself because she was unconsciously sabotaging her future at the company. After a few months of half-hearted work, she was put on a performance plan.

When you get stuck, you might feel so deep in your suffering that you can't see a way out. You may even get comfortable in your stuckness. This can happen for all kinds of reasons. Maybe you're uncomfortable asking for help. Maybe you don't believe you can get unstuck, so you stop trying. Maybe progressing scares you more than staying stuck does. Or maybe deep down, you don't believe you deserve to move forward. Caitlyn was soaking in a sea of her own anger and resentment, and the more stuck she got, the less motivated she felt to get out.

In one of our sessions, I broached the subject of her feeling so trapped. "I can feel how deep you are in your anger. But I think you've invested so much time and energy thinking you deserved that promotion that you can't seem to get past the fact that you didn't get it."

"Well, how do I get over it?" Caitlyn asked.

"I don't have a quick fix answer for you. But like a car stuck in the mud, if you keep hitting the gas, you're just going to keep spinning your wheels."

"Yeah, I get it," Caitlyn said. "But it's really unfair that I didn't get this promotion."

I went on. "Sometimes when we're overwhelmingly upset about one thing that's happened to us, it's because some of those feelings are really about other things that have happened to us. I wonder what else you might be feeling upset or angry about."

Caitlyn and I discussed how not getting this promotion reminded her of every other failure she'd ever experienced. We spoke about her fears that she would never accomplish anything. She cried tears of disappointment and anger and frustration and pain. I was proud of her for leaning into her emotions. But at some point, I realized Caitlyn needed help moving forward. And that help came in the form of a bit of tough love.

"Caitlyn, I can feel how devastating this situation has been for you. And I think we have some sense that some of your emotions aren't even about this promotion. But I also want you to ask yourself how long you're going to let this setback keep you from being the hardworking and determined person I know you to be. I want you to consider that, at this point, it might be *you* who's holding you back from getting to where you want to go."

Caitlyn looked a bit shocked, and she sat quietly with what I said. In that moment (and because of the extensive work she'd done on her mindfulness, curiosity, and self-awareness), she realized that it was time to pull herself out of the spiral. She understood that her behaviors were counterproductive to her success and happiness at work, and so together, we started to work on how she could get un-stuck and move forward. Unlike Ari, Caitlyn had felt every drop of her emotions, but like Ari, she hadn't really let herself grieve. She needed to grieve for expectations not met, dreams not achieved, and accomplishments not recognized, and then, she needed to take what she'd learned and keep marching forward. One of my favorite psychologists, Adam Phillips, said, "We share our lives with the people we have failed to be." To fully step toward the person you will become, you have to acknowledge and let go of the person you won't.

The Importance of Grief

There's a reason why most cultures have ceremonies and rituals around loss and grief—they honor something that has been lost and call in the community to help us get through it. They provide an opportunity to pause and acknowledge the loss, but also offer closure—when the ceremony is over, the next phase begins. Learning to grieve is one of the most powerful tools for resilience that there is. With it, you won't get stuck, nor will you pretend like things are fine when they're not. You will pause and honor your reality, and then you'll move forward. The key to resilience is finding your way toward a healthy middle, mid-pendulum swing—not too far over to the left where you don't allow yourself to feel, like Ari, nor too far over to the right like Caitlyn, where you're drowning in your emotions and can't get unstuck.

This is a process that's worth leaning into for every loss, even the small ones. Even the ones you've actively chosen. Early in my career, I received two exciting opportunities. One was a public speaking engagement in front of a community of people I deeply respected. The second was to teach a class alongside a cherished professor. Here was the problem, though: both were slated for the same day, on opposite sides of the country. I couldn't believe my luck to have been given both opportunities, but I also couldn't believe that I would have to turn one down. At dinner that evening, I was sitting with my friend Tim, feeling frustrated that I couldn't do both. When Tim asked what was wrong, I downplayed it.

"I can't believe I'm moping over this. Like, aw, poor me, I have two great opportunities. Sorry that I'm sitting here complaining about this champagne problem."

Tim cut me off. "Hey, don't do that to yourself. Don't belittle your feelings. It's okay that you feel disappointed. It sucks that you have to say no to something you really want to do, even if it allows you to say yes to something else. Here's an idea—how about you give yourself until the end of dinner to feel sad about whichever opportunity you're going to pass on, then let yourself get excited about the one you're going to choose while we eat dessert?"

My friend's permission to feel disappointed was incredibly

freeing. I was so grateful to sit with him and feel down about something that most people would call an abundance of riches. And in doing that, I was able to make a choice between the two opportunities, grieve the one I let go of, and be authentically excited for the one I took.

This might seem like a small or silly example of grief, but life is a constant stream of small losses: the lunch spot you were excited about is closed, a friend cancels plans you were looking forward to, your bonus is less than what you imagined it would be. You are constantly making choices—roughly thirty-five thousand each day, according to the experts, some as small as deciding what to eat for dinner and some as large as deciding on a job offer. Sometimes those choices are exciting, other times they're painful. Sometimes they feel insignificant, other times they feel deeply consequential. But there will always be choices. And with any choice made comes a choice (or many choices) lost. One of the most difficult but important realizations I had in adulthood is that there are rarely "right" or "wrong" choices in life, just different paths to take. With every choice you make, you have to grieve the loss of all you didn't get or choose. In this way, growth and grief are inextricably intertwined. Strengthen your ability to grieve, and your resilience will grow in ways you never thought possible. Pushing through failure and loss is a necessary skill, but the ability to face reality head-on, grieve, and heal is what refuels the grit tank for the next lap of the race.

GO AHEAD, GRIEVE

Remember that pendulum swing between avoiding your pain and getting stuck in it? If you try to move through a loss too quickly, you may set yourself up for another one; if you wallow in it for too long, you risk getting stuck there. So let's take what you learned about mindfulness and being uncomfortable and sit with a loss to find that sweet spot of resilience.

First, think of the last thing you lost. This might be something you had and then lost or something you hoped for but never got. Was it a job offer? A big client? An apartment? A second date? Next, list the emotions you're experiencing around that loss. Do you feel anger? Frustration? Resentment? Did your self-esteem take a hit? Maybe you started to question your abilities, and that has brought up anxiety. Check in with your body—where are you feeling these emotions? Where might they be stuck or hiding?

Witness your difficult emotions without judgment. Ask, "How can I best support myself in this moment? What do I need?" If it feels overwhelming, call on a friend, a loved one, or a therapist to sit with you in it. And when you're ready, I want you to have a little ceremony to offer a sense of closure. This could involve writing a letter to no one about anything you're feeling, that you then burn. You might light a candle and as you watch the flames, speak your frustrations into it, and watch them waft away. For bigger losses, perhaps you set up an annual ritual that reminds you to think about and honor that loss each year. Your ceremony can be anything that gives you permission to feel but also gives you the power to move through this tough time and feel some closure. Finally, write down the lessons you might take from the experience. How did the loss change you? What did it create space for? What did you learn about yourself and your life? Remember, a relationship, job, or experience does not have to last forever for it to have been worth having or doing.

You can also grieve proactively. Have you heard the term *sunk-cost fallacy*? It's when you're reluctant to abandon a strategy or decision because you've already invested a lot into it, even if it's clear that changing course would be more beneficial to you. This can be as simple as finishing a movie you don't like because you paid for the ticket, or as thorny as staying at a job you hate because you've been there for so long. I see it all the time with founders who refuse to pivot start-up ideas that aren't working because they worry that they've gone too far and would lose too much if they start down a new path.

Think of something in your life that you've been hesitant to abandon because of all you've invested into it. You might be hanging on to an unhealthy friendship because you've known them so long, or hanging on to a career you aren't passionate about because you worry about starting over. Now take some time to mourn the lost time, money, or effort that you've put into this thing. This can be as simple as just acknowledging to yourself that it's hard to let it go. You might talk about it in therapy, journal about it, or just say to yourself, *Damn! I wish I'd known this earlier, but I didn't. I made the best choice I could at the time.* As poet Maya Angelou said, "Forgive yourself for not knowing what you didn't know before you learned it."

Finally, get curious with yourself about what choice you want to make moving forward. Do you really want to keep going down this path? Or would it be better for you to change course? If you decide that changing course is the better choice, figure out how you can take the first step to make that happen. Don't forget to make room to grieve the loss—it's okay to feel sad even as you make a choice that feels right.

As Ari and I worked together, we talked about the emotional risk of plowing full steam ahead with his new company: the possibility of repeating the same mistakes, the real chance of burnout (which financially would be devastating), and his increasing anxiety. He gave himself a small break from worrying about his current company so he could unpack his experience with the last one. This afforded him the time to be sad, angry, and disappointed. And then, to help him with the important step of closure, I suggested he write a letter: to forgive himself for the loss of his first company, reflect on all he'd learned, and explore what he hoped would come next. He did, and then some: he also made amends with the people he had let down during that time and thanked them for sticking with him. As he honored what he had been through, he cleared space to enter the next chapter of his life in a more authentic and open way.

Obstacles to Resilience

There are several hurdles that can thwart your efforts to become more resilient, much like there are setbacks that can stymie your physical training. Where you might get a strained muscle or sprained ankle in the gym, emotional hurdles can make emotional fitness feel impossible. Let's talk about a few of these obstacles and how to navigate them:

ANXIETY

Do you often worry about what tomorrow will bring? Do you ruminate on things that may or may not happen? Do you rush out to meet your suffering and suffer future pain unnecessarily? If you're nodding your head, you're in good company. According to the US Census Bureau Household Pulse Survey, in 2023, nearly one in three adults experienced anxiety or depression symptoms (which seems . . . strangely low?). But the message is clear, anxiety is common. And it isn't particular in its targets: some of the greatest minds, from Abraham Lincoln to Oprah Winfrey, have experienced debilitating anxiety. But anxiety does serve a purpose—it helps you prepare for the things you might face in the future, like financial woes or an upcoming presentation that you should really practice for. According to the Yerkes–Dodson Law, you want just enough anxiety to be useful. Too little anxiety and you may not feel motivated enough to do something; too much, and you are so anxious you can't think of anything else.

Being resilient through anxiety is tough, but through practice (and practice again!) it can be strengthened. Remember my story about learning to trust my future self? That was one of the most powerful tools I added to my anxiety tool kit. Another one is remembering to focus on the things that I can control and to breathe and let go of the things that I can't. This may seem really obvious, but anxiety is a tricky little thing—it can convince you that if you worry enough, the bad thing *might* not happen—even if you don't actually have any control over that thing. So, at the same time that you want to stop worrying, you might cling to it for fear that if you stop, your greatest fears will come true. To move through anxiety, you'll have to let go of the fantasy that you have control over things you don't. Try this: the next time you're anxious about something, make a list of all of the factors involved, cross off the ones you don't have any control over, and make a plan for the ones you do.

If your anxiety is seriously disrupting your life, here's another tool to use: the worry hour. Whether it's obsessive thinking or just feeling wildly distracted by your anxiety, sometimes worry can outstay its welcome. When you find yourself in this state, consider scheduling a date night with your worries (it's a cheap date, I promise). Whether it's five minutes a day, a half hour per week, or an hour a month, set aside some time for worrying, obsessing, perseverating, and ruminating all you want. But—and here's the important part—the rest of the time, when you feel your worries pop up, remind yourself that that's a worry-hour problem. If you find yourself slipping, remember that future self? Write a reminder to them so that they can pick up at the designated worry hour where you're leaving off. That version of you will deal with it, so you can return to what you were doing.

YOUR INNER CRITIC

Each and every one of us has an inner voice that has developed over time. And sometimes, that inner voice is more like an inner bully. While it can be pretty tough to quiet your inner critic completely, don't let the voice that says *You're not enough* or *You can't handle it* be the only voice in your head. Summon your wiser, healthier self to say, *That's not the whole story.*

If you have trouble doing this, you might be struggling with confidence to face your tough feelings, confidence in your ability to handle the problem at hand, confidence in the options you have available to you, or confidence that you don't need to be perfect to be successful or loved. Every single person struggles with confidence in one form or another, at one time or another. But you can be your own biggest cheerleader. As author and coach Lisa M. Hayes says, "Be careful how you talk to yourself, because you are listening." Practice talking to yourself with more kindness and encouragement. It might feel contrived at first, but you will start to believe it over time.

For Caitlyn, it was hard to see past her anger, but once she did, she could admit to herself that underneath it all, her ego was bruised. Not getting the promotion ignited a whole set of feelings about not being good enough, which led to her perpetuating her worst fears by not showing up as her best self. Once she realized this, we were able to pull her out of the cycle and work on (a) speaking to herself with more kindness and compassion and (b) learning to see her struggles as an opportunity. We dissected her current position.

"You know, Caitlyn, it sounds like you're really good at your job. But maybe it just wasn't the right time for the promotion. Sometimes it's better to move up slowly than get thrown in over your head."

She was able to see my perspective. If she'd been promoted and then failed, she'd be much worse off. By staying at her current position, she was set up for success: working for a company she loves, in an industry she adores, with a cushion of time to gain experience.

Of course, not every setback has to be a positive force in your life. Everything does not always have to be "for the best." It's okay if a painful experience didn't make you stronger. It's okay if you're angry about a trauma, and not grateful for how it shaped you. Sometimes things are just shitty. And that's okay. Surviving is enough.

BURNOUT

Trying to be resilient when you're burned-out is like trying to get in shape by not eating. You need food to fuel your body to do the exercise it needs to get into shape. It's extremely common for people to walk into my office on the brink of total collapse, having waited until it felt like everything was falling apart to seek support. But by then, they have less internal resources to do the work. As is true with most of our struggles, burnout is so much easier to prevent than it is to fix. You have to give your mind and body what they need in order to face the inevitable struggles that life will throw at you. And you need to do that *before* the struggles hit. Here is a three-step plan for preventing burnout.

STEP 1: Identify your early burnout warning signs. What signs and signals indicate that burnout is around the corner? In other words, what happens to you when you *start* to get tired or overwhelmed? It might be that you're less patient with people in your life, or complain more, or get less or lower-quality sleep. It might be that you are less social, that you feel less content about your work, or that you lose your appetite. Note what these signs are for you and write them down.

STEP 2: Recruit support to keep an eye out for your early warning signs. Once you know what your early burnout signs are, share them with people in your life—your spouse, colleagues, best friend—and ask them to help you keep an eye out for them. Give them permission to check in on you if they notice that you're exhibiting these behaviors.

STEP 3: When you identify a warning sign, refuel. This is the most important step: when you or someone you've recruited notices an early burnout signal (or two), immediately schedule an activity (or three) that refuels your tank. This might be taking a mental health day, going for a walk in nature with your dog, putting some time on the calendar to see a close friend, or blocking off some time to be alone—whatever helps you feel more centered.

Note: When you do take time to refuel (something you should do regularly), you can't just take the time—you have to actually *enjoy* the time. Because if you don't leave the break feeling recharged, what's the point? Approach rest with the same intention and commitment that you bring to your work. Schedule it in advance. Stay off your email. Truly allow yourself to relax. Don't feel guilty about taking the break. Your work life will benefit, your mind and body will thank you, and your colleagues will be just fine.

By taking your early warning signs seriously and refueling before you've run completely out of gas, you'll be able to travel much further in your work and life.

SHAME

Shame can be a formidable enemy of resilience because it makes you think that you are unable or unworthy of moving forward into bigger and better things. And if you don't believe you can accomplish something or don't believe you are worthy of having it, you will find all kinds of creative (and often unconscious) ways to move away from the very things you most want. People with a lot of shame tend to use the word *should* with themselves way too often—meaning, they believe they *should* have been able to accomplish, change, or become something already. But if you think you already *should* have done something, it will keep you from believing that you *could* do it now. I like to remind my clients to "stop shoulding all over yourself." Instead of "should have" try "could have." For example, if you find yourself thinking, *I should have worked last night instead of watching TV*, stop yourself and say, *I could have worked last night, but I chose to watch TV to get some rest. Tonight, I'll focus on my work.* Overall, shame is a complicated emotion to clear away, and if you find yourself grappling with a lot of shame, I highly recommend bringing in support to work through it—for example, talking with a therapist or reading more about shame (see the resources section of this book for recommendations).

TOXIC POSITIVITY

If you were to look at just a few posts on social media, you would think the best way to face adversity is with a smile and a sunny affirmation. So often, people are told to be more resilient—by bosses who ask everyone to return to the office after the pandemic, by society that downplays marginalized people's concerns with institutional inequality, by the media that sets the standard for moms to be perfect at home *and* at work—but often what is really being requested is for people to suffer more quietly. Remember, resilience does not mean staying positive all the time. It doesn't mean not crying, not being affected by tough things, or not caring what people think. Our culture prefers avoidant quick fixes over uncomfortable but lasting healing. Toxic positivity is to resilience what diet pills are to exercise. They offer the fantasy of a quick and easy remedy but cause more problems in the long run. Think about that.

FEAR OF SUCCESS

It's ironic, but a fear of success can be as debilitating as a fear of failure. We are sometimes most afraid of the things we most want. Sometimes success feels like failure on a bigger platform (because there's further to fall). Whether it's because success would mean that things will change or because on some level you believe you don't deserve it (see *Shame*, on the previous page), you may subconsciously slow your ambitions.

Corey, a young go-getter I worked with years ago, was one of the first employees at a promising start-up. All the employees burned the oil well past midnight to make it successful, and they were an amazing team. Corey really loved his job; at this small venture, he wore many hats and enjoyed seeing all the angles of the company's inner workings. After years of hard work, the very thing he'd been pushing for finally happened: the company was acquired by a bigger corporation. Overnight, Corey was siloed to work on only one type of job all the time. He missed working closely with his friends, and he felt like a small cog in a big wheel at a huge company where no one really knew or cared much about him. Feeling isolated and diminished, he quit. He went and started working at a new start-up, thinking that it would be like "old times." But he noticed that he secretly hoped that this start-up wasn't as successful, because he hated all the loss he experienced when the last start-up succeeded. He was working against the very thing that he wanted. Together, Corey and I examined his idea of success, and he confronted his fears of change.

This concept dovetails into an interesting phenomenon that I see happen as people progress in their resilience: they sometimes sabotage their own progress without realizing it, because getting better now means facing that things could have been better a long time ago. It's the realization that, *Wait, if I could get better now, does that mean I could have been better this whole time?* If you can have a healthy relationship now, does that mean that you could have had a healthy relationship ten years ago? That question can be so painful that you convince yourself that it's just not possible to have it at all. So you sabotage your progress. It probably doesn't make a whole lot of sense that you would do something so damaging to yourself, but it's much more common than you think.

Like Corey, you may sometimes worry about what success will change in your life. The more agile you are in recognizing your feelings, the better you will be at pivoting back on track.

Resilience Push-Up: The Resource Inventory

All of these issues—anxiety, burnout, shame, toxic positivity, fear of success—are difficult to confront and change if you don't have a support system in place, and a good support system includes a diverse set of resources. To be your most resilient self, you'll want to pull out key resources from within yourself (internal) and from others (external). But it tends to be harder to remember what your resources are when you need them the most. For your resilience push-up, I want you to build what I call a resource inventory, where you'll take stock of the assets you can call on in a pinch.

A Cheat Sheet to Being More Resilient

Resilience isn't a light switch—it's not that you have resilience or you don't—how resilient you are in any given moment will depend on the context of the situation you're facing, where you are emotionally, and what resources you have. Remember, so much of your suffering comes from being stuck in your pain, or resisting your pain. Use these as reminders as you work on your resilience:

1. Acknowledge that setbacks, struggles, and pain are inevitable parts of life. You can't ignore them away.

2. Allow yourself to feel your emotions and remind yourself that you have gone through tough things before. Don't forget to grieve.

3. Offer yourself compassion and patience while being accountable for your actions. The most important lessons in life usually need to be learned over and over again (if you've ever gone back to an unhealthy relationship a few times, you know what I mean). It's okay to fail multiple times, you only need to get up one more time than you fall.

4. Lean into gratitude. Gratitude is a really powerful tool for resilience. It gets you through your anxiety and brings you back to the present moment. It reminds you what you still have and allows you to appreciate what you had before you lost it.

STEP 1: Think of a challenge or difficult situation that you're navigating right now. Perhaps you're feeling apathetic about your work or you're arguing a lot with your partner.

STEP 2: Whether you tend to avoid or get stuck in your challenges, you might not know that you already have an arsenal of **internal resources** you can pull from. Internal resources are the tools, perspectives, lessons, and mindsets you have cultivated over time and can draw on when needed. Take out a paper and pen or your laptop, and write down all of the internal resources you could tap into that would help you through your tough time. Some examples of internal resources include:

- the capacity to feel your tough feelings and tolerate discomfort (ahem, mindfulness and curiosity);

- the propensity to give yourself credit for previous challenges you've overcome and feel confident in your abilities;

- the ability to ask questions to best determine your options and choices;

- permission to be imperfect, permission to learn, and permission to rest;

- lessons you've learned from past struggles;

- a recognition of all you have going for you (gratitude).

STEP 3: I get it; it's tough to ask for help. You may find it hard to lean on others (no one wants to feel like a burden) or tell people you're struggling. But building your resilience alone is like trying to lift heavy weights without a spotter. The spotter's job is to help the lifter take proper form and safely complete the set without injury. Your community is an important source of strength, and people like to feel helpful and will likely be eager to help and support you. In this step, write down all the **external resources** you could tap into as you navigate your way through your tough moment. Some examples of external resources include:

- *Community.* This is your family and friends, your neighbors, your colleagues, and the role models who support you in your growth. They've been there before and understand you and your challenges. Write down every single person you could call on if you needed them.

- *Mentors.* People lucky enough to find mentors can enormously benefit from such a valuable source of emotional support during tough times. Not only do they offer an incredibly empathetic perspective, but they can share how they navigated their own difficulties and setbacks.

- *Formal support (therapy and educational resources).* No matter how large and loving your circle of friends, family, and mentors is, there is no substitute for a good therapist who can offer educated and objective advice. Short of that, classes and books from experts can provide a mountain of information and indirect support; memoirs from people who have walked through their own struggles can inspire you to shore up your own resilience.

Once you know what these external resources are, don't hesitate to make use of them. If you have trouble asking for help then all the external resources in the world won't help you.

Human beings do not exist in isolation. We are communal creatures, and we all need support.

STEP 4: Review your list of internal and external resources. Is it short? Long? How do you feel about it? How might you make use of your internal and external support to get through the challenge you're facing? Are there resources you might add to your arsenal?

Now that you have this list, you can look at it whenever you need a reminder that you can do hard things. Of course, becoming resilient won't happen overnight, but with the right tools and headspace, it's a muscle you can flex every time a new challenge comes your way. Once you do build up your own coffers, you will be able to expand that wealth into helping others. Resilient people seek balance, supporting themselves while looking out for other people. As you become more resilient, you'll be better able to put yourself in another person's shoes and understand their feelings and needs. It's an incredible skill to have, that capacity to be with people where they are. That's **empathy**, and that is the next chapter.

7
EMPATHY
Understanding Others

Empathy is about finding echoes of another person in yourself.

—MOHSIN HAMID

Will was overwhelmed.

"I'm just not used to so much . . . hand-holding . . . ," he confided in me in one of our early sessions. He was wrestling with how to manage a spat between two of his reports—a new experience for him. After spending many years as a highly skilled engineer in a thriving IT company in New York City, Will had recently been promoted and whisked away from his individual-contributor (IC) role in Manhattan to oversee a team of engineers in their West Coast office. And while he was still tasked with some coding work, leading a team (for the first time in his career) would be his primary job. He was a fantastic engineer, but having eight people working under him, he knew he would need to build his managerial chops.

"Brian has been complaining to me that Jordan isn't a team player. Which is true, but then he started talking about how he doesn't get the recognition at the company that Jordan does and that they used to be friends but now they're not. . . . I don't know, it's clear that there's some bad blood between them that I'm not privy to, but it's making meetings super tense. So I told Brian, 'Honestly, all of that isn't really my problem. Work it out between the two of you. This is work. It isn't kindergarten.'"

While I understood Will's desire to focus on the work, I offered another perspective. "I can definitely understand your hesitance to dive into all of that with them. But, there's a big difference between being an IC and being a manager, and that is that the interpersonal dynamics of your team are now, at least in part, your problem. A rift between two of your reports that's affecting their work is something you'll need to address if you want to be an effective leader." I realized that my work with Will, as he grew into his new role, would likely center around helping him develop some empathy.

When I say *empathy*, I'm referring to the ability and willingness to actually *feel* what someone else is feeling in order to understand and respond to them. Most people don't realize that empathy has an emotional component: if you *intellectually* understand what someone else is feeling but *you're* not feeling it yourself, that is not empathy—that's *sympathy*. And while empathy has traditionally been viewed as a necessary skill for those in "service" professions, such as medicine, education, and caregiving, increasingly, it's being recognized as a critically important skill everywhere. Business of any kind is really just a series of relationships, and in any relationship, empathy is a key ingredient for success. And whether it's an employee silently coping with a chronic illness, or that seemingly coolheaded manager who struggles with their self-confidence, *everyone* is fighting an internal battle you don't know about.

Will, who had become a stellar engineer because of his finely tuned rational thinking, was not overflowing with empathy, but it was clear to me that he was capable of it. And for the sake of his new role, he felt motivated to work on it. Unfortunately, he didn't have many mentors to model himself after. His bosses in New York were cut from the same cloth as he was and tended to tune out any emotional display, and he'd grown up in a family and culture that promoted having a "stiff upper lip."

This new environment felt like a different world to Will. The laxer West Coast culture was definitely a factor, but it also had a lot to do with his team: he was working with a younger generation who were much more open to emoting at work. Some might say that Gen Z is *too* touchy-feely, but their generation should be credited for bringing empathy to the conversation in the modern workplace. To quote future of work expert Adam Smiley Poswolsky, "Gen Z is the meaning-making generation." Millennials and Gen Z are the first generations in living memory to grow up to be *less* wealthy than their parents. Faced with the reality that they will be expected to work the same number of hours their parents did (or more) but unlikely to be able to afford a similar lifestyle (like buying a house), the desire to feel like their work has *purpose* has taken on new importance.

A few sessions later, Will came to me with a similar "feelings" situation (yes, he used air quotes). One of his reports, Kari, was having trouble at home—she was caring for a sick parent and a young child all while trying to excel at work. Kari had come to Will to share her situation, and Will didn't know what to do with it.

"Don't get me wrong, it sounds like Kari's life is hard right now. But in my last role, we were focused on the work, and everyone dealt with their own shit. Suddenly I feel responsible for Kari and everything going on in her world, and I'm in over my head."

I took a second to process what Will was saying.

"That sounds tough," I said. "And maybe a little overwhelming?

I can definitely imagine what it must feel like to step into this new role ready to support your team's work, only to feel like you're drowning in all their emotions."

"Right? Exactly. Thank you."

"I'm curious, Will. How did it feel just now to hear me say that I understand where you're coming from?"

"Oh . . . I mean, good, I guess. Seems like you get it."

"I do. I get where you're coming from because I took a second to really feel what you might be feeling. I put myself in your shoes and felt your frustration and overwhelm. And I'm sharing this because I wonder what it would be like for you to do some of that with your reports."

"Okay, but you're my therapist. I'm not Brian's therapist, or Jordan's therapist, or Kari's therapist."

"You're right that you're not their therapist, and it's not your job to coddle or fix their feelings. But we all bring our emotions with us to work whether we like it or not, and whether you like it or not. If you can let yourself at least *understand* their experience, you'll be in a much better position to support them. And in order to understand their feelings, you'll have to let yourself feel them, at least a little bit."

"Okay. That's fair. But how do I do that?"

Why Empathize?

Empathy is so crucial for healthy relationships that Stanford University psychologist Dr. Jamil Zaki labeled empathy as the "psychological 'superglue' that connects people." It's been shown time and time again that empathy significantly increases understanding, trust, and connection, which in turn improves the overall satisfaction of a relationship. And this empathy "superglue" really *is* sticky.

In one study, researchers assigned advanced dementia patients with two caretakers: one would treat them with empathy and kindness, and the other would be cold and unloving (but not abusive). After a week, the patients were asked if they had ever met either of the two caretakers. They all said no (because of the dementia), but when they were asked who they wanted to work with that day, they consistently chose the caretaker who had treated them kindly, even though they couldn't explain why they made this choice. The researchers used this study to surmise that emotional memory is encoded and stored differently than our logistical memory. To me, it's a reminder that in life, people may forget what you said, but they won't forget how you made them *feel*.

Empathy is just as powerful in the workplace. An empathetic boss is more likely to create an environment in which employees feel valued and understood. Such an environment can lower stress and anxiety levels, as well as build trust and collaboration. In one study, 86 percent of participants felt they were better able to handle work and life pressures when they felt supported by an empathetic boss (wouldn't you prefer to work with someone who seeks to understand your experience and weighs your needs alongside their own?) Empathy also fosters more empathy. When people see it in action, they're more likely to reciprocate, with you and with others around them.

This trickle-down effect can have a huge impact on productivity in so many ways. One study showed that when people felt that their leaders were empathetic, they reported being more creative and innovative (61 percent of employees compared to only 13 percent of employees with less empathetic leaders). And this ability to be creative, innovative, and empathetic is especially important when it comes to the ideation of products and services. Think about it: every component of a service or product needs to consider user experience, and to know what a user needs, you must be able to empathize with them. Empathy leads to game-changing innovation. A few examples:

- OXO kitchen utensils: In the 1980s, Sam Farber, the founder of OXO, noticed his wife, Betsey, struggling with a vegetable peeler due to her arthritis. Sam and Betsy decided to design a new line of kitchen utensils with chunky, easy-to-grip handles that could be used comfortably by anyone, including those with limited dexterity. OXO's user-centric approach, born out of empathy, revolutionized the kitchenware industry and made cooking more accessible for people with disabilities.

- Patagonia: Retail founder Yvon Chouinard was an avid outdoorsman who empathized with the growing concern for sustainability among his customers. Chouinard pioneered the use of recycled materials and introduced initiatives like the Common Threads Partnership, which encourages customers to repair, reuse, and recycle their garments. Patagonia's empathy for its customers' values and the environment has made it a leader in sustainable fashion.

- Fenty Beauty: Pop icon Rihanna launched Fenty Beauty in 2017 with the goal of creating a cosmetics line for those underserved by traditional beauty products. "Fenty Beauty by Rihanna was created for everyone: for women of all shades, personalities, attitudes, cultures, and races. I wanted everyone to feel included." Fenty now boasts fifty foundation shades that cater to a wide range of skin tones and set a new standard for inclusivity in the beauty industry.

A Path to Empathy

While empathy is important to have, it is not always easy to develop. It comes naturally to some, others gain it over time, and many still struggle to develop it throughout their lives. Some people also feign empathy: ever meet a boss who openly touts his support of working moms only to reduce maternity leave? In some ways, empathy is a big ask—you might not always *want* to feel what someone else is feeling, and even if you do, you might not have been taught how.

There are a few factors that contribute to how empathetic you are. Biology and genetics play a role. A recent study showed that empathy is approximately 10 percent genetic, and that the rest is picked up from family and environment. Studies also indicate that women tend to exhibit greater empathy overall, which may stem from biological factors such as more naturally occurring oxytocin (the nurturing hormone responsible for bonding). However, sociocultural elements also likely contribute, given the enduring gender-role expectations prescribing women as caring and men as stoic. It's hard to shake off thousands of years of expectations for women to be nurturing and men to be less emotional.

Modern realities have also messed with our natural tendencies toward empathy. While technology has helped us connect to more people all around the world, in many ways we are more disconnected and isolated than ever. Between Zoom calls, Slacking, texting, not to mention AI chatbots, our lives are lived facing screens far more than each other. Empathy—really feeling what someone else is feeling—relies on cues like facial expressions, tone of voice, and body language, which are a lot harder to decipher through a phone or computer. For example, if you say something unkind in person, you're forced to witness and experience how it makes the other person feel (their face scrunches up, their eyes well up with tears, you can feel their hurt). If you type it into a comment section, though, you can act out your aggressive impulses without ever having to empathize with the consequences of your actions (and thus internet trolls abound). In this digital age, if you don't work actively to stay connected to other people, your natural muscle for empathy will atrophy.

Beefing Up Empathy

Ready to work on your empathy? If you've been doing your emotional push-ups, then you've got this. Growing your empathy will rely heavily on strengthening earlier traits in this book. Let's talk about how to use the skills you've been practicing so far to deepen the empathy you have for yourself and for others.

First, mindfulness. If you're uncomfortable feeling your own feelings, you'll avoid feeling anyone else's. Staying present in an emotional moment is tough for most people, but by tolerating the discomfort, you'll create space to truly listen and connect with other people.

Curiosity will help you to ask questions and understand diverse perspectives. Ask open-ended questions to learn more about other people's situations, backgrounds, and frames of reference. Soak it all up like a sponge before forming a response. You'll be surprised at how much more you grasp when you stay curious.

To identify other people's emotions and needs, you'll need to check in with yourself about your own. This is where self-awareness comes in. Make sure you're familiar with a wide range of emotions so that you can recognize what's coming up for you and the person you're empathizing with.

And, of course, it's tough to empathize with others when you're burnt out or stuck—you can't pour from an empty cup. The resilience you've built to get through your own difficult moments will help you support others through theirs.

One of the best ways you can strengthen your empathy is to expose yourself to as many different cultures and experiences as you possibly can. Columbia Business School professor Adam Galinsky has long studied the benefits of travel on the brain and believes that exploring new places increases our propensity for perspective-taking, which is critical to empathy. When you step outside of your normal life and immerse yourself in novel contexts, you're forced to look through a different lens. Simple acts like listening to a new genre of music, touring an unfamiliar neighborhood, or trying a new type of food, all provide eye-opening opportunities. The key is to go in with an open mindset and an eagerness to see the world through perspectives unlike your own. Remember Bourdain? His show was basically a master class in how curiosity fosters empathy. He took us across the globe to challenge our preconceived views of other cultures. Diverse experiences rewire your brain, making you a more flexible empath. Expand your horizons—watch a documentary, read a book, take a class, go somewhere new.

Where There's a Will There's a Way

Will had a lot of reps to do to develop his capacity for empathy. But it was a great sign that he wanted to be a good manager badly enough to commit to it. He started by flexing his curiosity and self-awareness. He paid closer attention to his emotions and kept a journal of them throughout the day. When did he feel frustrated, excited, anxious?

He challenged himself to get as specific as possible—he wasn't just happy, he was proud. He wasn't just sad, he was deflated. What triggered those emotions? Which emotions did he try to avoid in others and in himself? Will found that just noticing his internal experience allowed him to be more attuned to the emotional states of those around him. But he knew he needed to go further.

To flex his mindfulness, Will consciously practiced being more present when interacting with his team members, especially Brian, Jordan, and Kari. Instead of getting swept up in his own thoughts about the work at hand, he made an effort to stop, breathe, and actually look at them while they spoke. He noticed their facial expressions, body language, and tone of voice and used those cues to imagine what they might be feeling and needing. Finally, Will made sure he was well-resourced so that he had the energy and resilience to support his team. In addition to working with me, Will set up a quarterly meeting with his boss specifically to get support being a better leader, and he joined a group of engineering managers to commiserate with (turns out he wasn't the only rational-minded engineer in Silicon Valley).

Will reminded himself that just by caring about his team members, he was doing his job as a manager. When Jordan shot a dismissive look at Brian during a meeting, instead of ignoring it as he might have before, Will made a mental note to follow up.

"Brian, I'm curious how you're doing after that meeting. You shared a really helpful idea, and I don't think it was recognized. But I noticed, and I'm excited for the team to give it a try."

Though the process wasn't easy, over the next few months, Will made efforts like this again and again—staying self-aware, present, and curious about his team's interpersonal dynamics. He listened, validated feelings, and worked to help them understand each other's perspectives. He also made a point of trying new experiences that expanded his empathy. He attended company socials and happy hours that he might have skipped in the past, using them as opportunities to have authentic conversations with people from different backgrounds. He also picked up new hobbies like photography that helped him appreciate new perspectives in a creative way.

It wasn't an instantaneous transformation, but over time and with practice, Will's empathy muscle grew stronger. He became better at picking up on emotional cues, regulating his own responses, and building an environment of trust within his team. Interpersonal conflicts didn't magically disappear, but they caused less disruption as Will earned his team's trust in being someone who genuinely cared about their experiences, not just their output. More than just helping him be a better manager, developing empathy allowed Will to connect with others in a deeper way. It made him more resilient, more adaptable, and more fulfilled. And it set him up for continued growth as a leader who could bring out the best in those around him.

THE IMPORTANCE OF BOUNDARIES

Some of you might be reading this thinking, *But I'm the opposite of Will! I feel too much of what other people are feeling!* If you tend to empathize with others naturally, you may be wondering if it's possible to have too much empathy. You may feel the stress and burden of taking on more than your fair share of someone else's emotions. If there was any question about whether compassion fatigue existed, that question was answered during the pandemic, when millions of doctors, nurses, teachers, and other front-liners exhausted themselves into submission. Unrelenting stress and constant outpouring of care can trigger an "acute inability to empathize," which inhibits your thinking and emotions and can dampen hope. Like overexercising, your body can only take on so much. You need relief from that constant effort—it's like a rubber band that snaps when it's been stretched too far. For many, a world-halting pandemic isn't needed to reach their compassion limit. Whether you have a job that expects empathy-on-demand or you're a nurturer by default, you may feel like you have to Take. Care. Of. Everything. But it's important to remember, empathy is not about sacrificing what you want or need in order to make others happy. And empathy is not about letting people get away with everything or taking on their problems as your own. In my experience, when people feel like they have too much empathy, what is usually going on is that they don't have strong enough boundaries.

Anything that involves vulnerability requires boundaries. And boundaries are the healthiest way to deal with the fact that you can only control yourself. Boundaries make empathy possible, and without great and sturdy boundaries, an empathetic person will burn out fast. Therapy is a great example of the marriage between empathy and boundaries in action. As a therapist, it is my job to be deeply empathetic—to feel what my clients are feeling so I can understand them and help them better understand themselves. Over the course of fifty minutes, I take in everything they're feeling—their joy, their pain, their trauma. I might spend up to thirty hours a week doing this every week! But this relationship only works with boundaries, which is why therapy has many: We meet on the same day of the week in the same room, we start on time and end on time, and I don't see my clients socially or in any context outside of that room. Without these boundaries in place, I would get overwhelmed very quickly. If I thought that the session might last twice as long, or if I knew I was going to see that client at a party later that night, I wouldn't be able to go as deep with them. And because my clients know that I will hold my boundaries firmly, they are able to lean into their vulnerability in a deeper way. The stronger and more transparent my boundaries are, the deeper my empathy can go—the same will be true for you in all of your relationships.

If you are constantly helping or supporting others—whether at work or in your personal life—there will come a time when you *will* burn out if you don't set up boundaries. This would be doing yourself and your loved ones a disservice. Some empathetic people worry that if they say no, they are letting people down. But actually, offering only what you truly have available is one of the kindest things you can do for those in your life. By not letting people take too much or take advantage of you, you protect yourself, them, and the relationship. Think about kids or teens who aren't given any rules— those who have no bedtime, eat what they want, and don't have to call if they're going to be late—they may be grateful on the surface not to have boundaries, but deep down, these kids often feel unloved and uncared for, and they tend to have more behavioral problems than those who know that there are limits that are being upheld and enforced.

To create boundaries at work and at home, you'll need to flex that self-awareness muscle. What are your strengths and your limits? How much energy do you have for others without sacrificing the energy you need for yourself? What are you willing to put up with? What causes resentment for you if you allow it? Think about how to set up boundaries around these things. For example, if you're willing to start work early but need to be done at 5:00 p.m. every day to pick up your kids, it will be up to you to make that clear to your team, to put up an away message every evening, and to hold firm when people try to persuade you to take a late meeting. The discomfort you feel at saying no will pale in comparison to the resentment that will build if you say yes. If you have a friend who is constantly asking for favors, you might have to say, "I care about you and want to show up for you, and I don't have the capacity to do this particular favor for you." Though this might be hard for them to hear, you are ultimately protecting the relationship with your honesty.

If you are new to upholding boundaries, you might feel resistance at first from those in your life who aren't used to being told no. But I've found that people tend to adjust, and that in the long run, the relationship will be better off because everyone will have a clear understanding of what's available to them, and you will be less likely to grow resentful or exhausted by the relationship (and thus more able to be authentically empathetic within your boundaries). Take Will's scenario: he didn't know how to handle Kari's dilemma, so we talked through some choices. He set up a one-on-one with Kari to get a sense of what she was going through. Kari shared that her father was very ill, that she was co-parenting a five-year-old, and that she felt like she was flailing and failing at her job.

"How was it for you, listening to Kari in that way?" I asked him in one session.

"It was uncomfortable for sure. And I had to fight my urge to say, 'What am I supposed to do about that?' But I'm grateful that Kari felt comfortable letting me in. And understanding what she's going through does give me a better sense of how to support her. I took a few projects off her plate and reminded her that our office has free day care services that she can sign up for. The thing is, I'm not sure what the next step is. I can't fix her problems."

"I get that, Will. It's a lot to sit with. It sounds like you really empathized with her, though, and that she felt heard. From here, it's not actually your job to fix her problems at all. If you find her continuing to look for help that you can't give her, this is where setting boundaries comes in. You might tell her that you know she's going through a lot, but that you aren't the right person to support her. Refer her to HR, which will have the resources to get her some help—like talking to her own therapist. You might encourage her to use some vacation days in the meantime but steer her in the right direction for more support. Sound good?"

Will did just that, and once he figured out how to be a bit more empathetic with Kari, he began to see where he could be more empathetic in every aspect of his job—within boundaries, of course. As he better understood his staff's and colleagues' experience, he was able to better identify the pressures his team would be under to meet a deadline. He could rally the troops when they needed an extra push, and he could congratulate the team when a job was well executed. His team felt more supported and, in turn, were more productive and creative in their work.

Empathy for Yourself

As important as it is to empathize with others, it's also vital to turn your compassion inward. Most people are their own worst critic, especially when faced with tough challenges or mistakes. Having self-compassion means treating yourself with patience and kindness, and forgiving yourself for being an imperfect human. Self-compassion is not self-pity or wallowing, and it's not about lowering your standards. In fact, research shows that self-compassion fuels resilience, helps you bounce back faster from setbacks, and is linked to reduced anxiety, depression, and stress, as well as enhanced happiness, life satisfaction, and motivation. If you're hard on yourself—if you judge yourself harshly for perceived flaws or failures, you're likely to feel unmotivated and discouraged when you face setbacks.

Empathy for yourself means letting yourself feel your emotions, supporting yourself through difficult moments, and recognizing that imperfection is part of the human experience. To cultivate self-compassion, tune in to yourself regularly and flex a little mindfulness. Notice when you're engaging in harsh self-talk or judgment, and make an effort to treat yourself with as much love and care as you would a close friend. Use soothing language and acknowledge that you are doing the best you can.

Remember—it will never work to hate yourself into a better version of who you are.

Self-compassion also involves treating yourself with care, not just kind words. When you're having a hard time, ask, *How can I comfort and care for myself in this moment?* Maybe that looks like a walk, a chat with a supportive friend, or another soothing activity like reading or cooking your favorite comfort meal. By being a kind and encouraging ally to yourself, you'll equip yourself to take much better care of others in a sustainable way.

That being said, one pop-psychology trope I'd like to erase from the ethos is the very commonly shared idea that no one will love you until you learn to love yourself. I call bullshit on this one, because I know from the work I do that we learn to love ourselves through the love we receive from others, ideally starting with our caregivers when we're young. The truth is, you can't love yourself unless you have been loved and are loved. The capacity to love can't be built in isolation. Society pushes the idea that you should pull yourself up by your bootstraps and manifest things for yourself, even if you were never taught how to do that. But that's not really how love works. Instead, surround yourself with people who love you *while* you learn to love yourself. And, as your love for yourself grows, you will *also* attract and accept more love into your life from others.

Empathy Push-Up: The Emotional Fitness Survey

Research shows that we tend to empathize better with things we understand. Think back to the last time a friend or coworker was really annoying or frustrating you. Perhaps they were complaining a lot, turned in work late, or just seemed to be in a foul mood. You might have been completely fed up with them. But then, you got more context—maybe you found out that they recently lost a family member or pet, or that they were going through a divorce. Suddenly, you softened to their behavior—it likely became easier to understand and empathize with them because you know that you're not always on your best behavior when you're going through a tough time. For this reason, a powerful way to build empathy for others is to increase your understanding of who they are and what they need.

So, how do you figure out what your colleagues and loved ones need from you? One tool I often use in my corporate work is what I call the emotional fitness survey. The goal of this survey is to gather information about what people need in order to show up as their best selves and do their best work, and your push-up for empathy is to put together an emotional fitness survey of your own. Think of it as a handy reference guide to understand and anticipate people's needs so you can empathize with them when the time comes. Filling out this survey can be incorporated into the onboarding process for any new employee, or rolled out right now.

STEP 1: Make a list of questions that you'd like to have on your emotional fitness survey. Think about what kind of information will help you get to know the people you work and live closely with. Here are a few examples:

- Do you like to be praised in public or in private?

- Do you prefer feedback that is direct and blunt or gentle and kind?

- How do you like to be cared for or cheered up during a tough time?

- How would I know if you were upset or overwhelmed?

- What time of day do you do your best thinking?

- How do you like your birthday to be celebrated?

- Do you prefer to be supported closely or given space and freedom?

- What else would you like your colleagues to know about you?

The question *How would I know if you were stressed or overwhelmed?* will help you be a more empathetic teammate, manager, and friend. For example, let's say someone wrote on their survey that when they get stressed out, they tend to skip meals. And let's say you've noticed that they skipped lunch the last four days in a row. You may want to ask what's up or take something off their plate. The question *When do you do your best thinking?* is a great one to reference when you're scheduling a brainstorming session with someone. And the question *How do you like your birthday to be celebrated?* will clue you in to which of your reports is private about their birthday and doesn't want a big celebration when it rolls around, and which want it to be treated like a national holiday. Knowing more about the people you work and live with will help you show up for and empathize with them.

STEP 2: Create your emotional fitness survey using your list of questions. This can be done digitally: it's a cinch to generate and send a Google Form, and answers can be shared easily. Then fill out the survey yourself! You'll want to get a sense of how it feels to answer each question, and you'll set the tone for everyone else to answer honestly and vulnerably. Answering these questions and sharing your own emotional "user's manual" may feel strange initially, but that's what mindfulness, self-awareness, curiosity, and resilience are for.

This is a chance to get to know what other people need, but also to share what *you* need. For example, on my own survey, I acknowledged that because of my ADHD, I sometimes interrupt people without meaning to. I gave everyone who works with me permission to call me out on it when it happens. I wrote: "If I interrupt you, please stop me so you can finish your thought." This worked beautifully—after sending out my answers, I noticed that people who may have been uncomfortable saying something to me when I interrupted suddenly started speaking up, and it has made interactions that much more satisfying and productive.

STEP 3: Send the survey to a group of people in your life. This can be your team at work, or your family or group of friends. A few tips: Transparency is the name of the game here. Make sure people know, before they fill out the survey, exactly who will have access to the answers (only management? everyone at the company?). All questions should be optional. People might not feel comfortable answering certain questions, and it's their choice what they share. You should give everyone ongoing edit access to their answers, so that they can add, remove, or change their responses over time. Leadership should fill out the survey as well.

I've seen this survey come in handy more times than I can count. When one of our employees at Coa lost a loved one, we took a look at her emotional fitness survey answers (which she had filled out months before when she joined the company). With the question, "What do you need when you're going through a tough time?" she answered, "First, I need some space, and then you can come check on me." And so, we left her alone for a few days and then, when we felt the time was right, we reached out. If we hadn't collected that information in advance and had bombarded her with condolences and sympathies right away, we may have overwhelmed her. By knowing to give her space, we allowed her to grieve in her own way while still feeling supported by us.

Just by sending out a survey like this, you will demonstrate care and support. Of course you can't tailor every moment to each person's preferences, but you would be surprised how many issues can be prevented simply by knowing what your colleagues and loved ones need from you.

This is the right approach to empathy—because people are different. I am not a fan of the golden rule, "treat others as you would like to be treated," because that assumes that everyone else has the same needs and preferences as you do, and that's not always the case. Instead, the rule should be "treat others the way *they* need to be treated." Leaning into empathy will transform your relationships, and as you better understand your needs and boundaries, as well as the needs and boundaries of others, you'll be in a much better position to solve problems and collaborate through conflict. Of course, this requires good communication. So let's learn how to **communicate** more effectively.

8
COMMUNICATION
Speaking Truth

*I am so clever that sometimes I don't understand a
single word of what I am saying.*

—OSCAR WILDE

"So when Kyle asked if he could take lead on the next campaign,
again, you said . . ."

"Uh . . ." Stephanie gave me a guilty look and shifted uncomfort-
ably in her seat.

"Hmm . . . I know what that look means. You said that it's fine."

"Yeah, I said that it's fine."

"But it's not fine."

"No, it's not fine. He headed up the last two campaigns, and he's
barely been working here a year. Why should I have to take a back
seat just so Kyle can feel important?"

"Well, you shouldn't have to take a back seat. You were promoted because of your experience. So why do you think you said yes
when Kyle asked to take the lead?"

"Because I hate saying no."

"I know you do. You hate saying no, but . . . you also hate being
sidelined. And I think you might be starting to hate Kyle, too."

"Ugh. You're not wrong."

Stephanie had been working at a high-end beauty brand for more than ten years, starting as an entry-level coordinator and rising to become a senior marketing director, and she couldn't imagine working anywhere else. Her personality was suited for it: she was ambitious, smart, and intuitive, and it was a relatively easy transition into a senior role—her colleagues trusted her and her campaigns succeeded. But she had one Achilles' heel: as a lifelong people pleaser, Stephanie struggled to say no. It didn't help that many of her colleagues had worked at the company for as long as she had and remembered her as the young eager-to-please assistant who got them coffee. Her boss and teammates regularly stepped over her unstated, unenforced boundaries: Could she stay late to work on the budget? Could she spell-check the deck for the next morning's meeting? Could she work on Saturday . . . again? These tasks were not her responsibility, but each time she acquiesced. She didn't want to disappoint anyone, so she said yes with a smile. Privately, though, she seethed. And over time, she grew resentful. In seemingly random moments, she would lash out at people in her life, damaging her relationships for reasons she nor they understood. Talk about not letting people down—she threw them off the roof instead.

Stephanie's story is not unique. Many people, raised to be accommodating team players, struggle to advocate for themselves. They contort into psychological pretzels, rationalizing away their needs until they're depleted, resentful husks. Without the ability to clarify expectations and set boundaries, they are forever at the mercy of others' demands. Other people have the opposite problem— they make their needs *extremely* known but don't communicate them clearly, thoughtfully, kindly, or proactively—in other words, they don't communicate their needs in a way that allows others to understand or want to accommodate them.

Our next trait, communication, is the ability to accurately, directly, and thoughtfully share your feelings, boundaries, needs, and expectations with others. If you are unable to communicate, have tough conversations, and work through conflict collaboratively, it will be nearly impossible to have deep and sustained relationships in your life. Connection does not exist without communication—it's what holds relationships together. But direct communication can be challenging for a slew of reasons—fear of disrupting a relationship, a lack of self-confidence, a shaky understanding of what your needs and expectations even are. Many people lack the skill simply because they didn't and don't have any role models who showed what good communication looks like.

Not to mention, communication has gotten a lot more complicated in the past couple of decades, with so much of it being done virtually. Not only do you need to be able to have generative conversations face-to-face, you now also need to know how to convey your ideas, emotions, and needs screen-to-screen, and through text. These days, an average of twenty hours per week are spent communicating digitally, and nearly 50 percent of people say their productivity is affected by what they consider poor communication. This way of connecting is here to stay, though, so let's address how to show up both physically and virtually.

Clearing the Air

There are a lot of things we don't talk about when we should. I've seen people wait to ask for a promotion until they're on the verge of quitting. I've seen couples avoid talking about money even as they legally merge finances. I've seen people end relationships of all kinds without a single conversation about what needed to change. Emotional fitness is all about approaching things proactively instead of reactively, and communication is no exception. Honest communication can be uncomfortable, so those who have not been flexing their mindfulness muscles might go to great lengths to avoid it.

Often the justification for avoiding a conversation is that it "isn't a big deal."

I'm just disappointed, you might think. *It doesn't seem worth it to say anything.* In other words: you downplay and dismiss your emotions and needs. The problem with this? Disappointment that isn't expressed calcifies into resentment, and resentment is a hell of a lot harder to clear away than disappointment. Whether you are disappointed that your partner didn't remember your anniversary or a work colleague forgot to include you on an important email, you may think you're protecting them by not letting them know how you feel, but really you are doing yourself, them, and your relationship a huge disservice. By communicating things as they happen, you'll keep small problems from becoming big problems. Regular, proactive communication is like brushing your teeth to avoid the buildup of emotional plaque. And when you can put words to your needs, boundaries, and expectations, they are so much more likely to be met.

People also avoid communicating because they feel everyone in their life should be able to read their mind and *just know* what they need. One example I hear: "If I ask my boyfriend to take me out on more dates, and then he does, then the dates don't count because he's only doing it because I asked him to." Does this sound familiar? Your loved ones and colleagues are not mind readers—if you ask for something and then receive it, that is an act of care and support. One of the best things you can do for your relationships is to figure out what your needs are (self-awareness check) and then ask for them. When you tell people what you want and need, you'll be surprised by what you get.

Workin' on Your Fitness

There's a reason why communication is our sixth trait. It's hard work. The act of communicating what you feel with other people is a heavy lift. Prepare yourself. While communicating will help you build your overall emotional fitness, it's a tough skill to develop without strength in the other traits you've been working on so far. Let's talk about how each muscle you've been flexing will help you be a better communicator.

> **Mindfulness:** Communicating effectively, especially during times of conflict, is uncomfortable, especially if you haven't been taught or empowered to practice it. But it's important to remind yourself that you are likely to endure all kinds of discomfort by *not* communicating. An uncomfortable conversation with your colleague about how you can collaborate better will be more manageable than the feeling of silently hating them day in and day out. The discomfort of letting your new romantic partner know that quality time is important to you is likely easier to overcome than constantly second-guessing the relationship. When it's time to have a tough conversation, remind yourself that you can handle it, and that you are worthy of having your needs heard and met.

Curiosity: To communicate effectively, you must first lower your defenses. Honest communication is a two-way street— it's a dance between you and the person or people you're communicating with. Curiosity allows for a conversation to go in both directions—it helps you ask questions to understand another person's position *and* take in what is being offered back to you. The more authentically curious you are, the better at communicating you'll be.

Self-awareness: How could you expect yourself to communicate wants and needs that you don't even know you have? It's important to get clear about your intentions before communicating them. What are you feeling? Why might you be feeling that way? What are you hoping to get out of a conversation with someone? Understanding your communication style and what is or isn't working about it is an important first step to improving it. Do you tend to be too timid? Too aggressive? Unclear? Unkind? Spend some time thinking about when your conversations go well and when they don't go so well.

Resilience: Not all communication is going to be positive. You're likely to experience adversity, conflict, and people who have not been working on their emotional fitness like you have. Resilience will support you through these moments and will ensure that you are in touch with the internal and external resources you'll need to collaborate with others effectively.

Empathy: People are much more likely to take in (and care about) what you're saying if they feel connected to you emotionally. Communicating with empathy means having some understanding of the other person's feelings and needs. Communicating your boundaries will serve as a crucial guardrail around your needs and expectations. Since only you know your boundaries, you'll need to tell other people what they are and enforce them when crossed. If you don't, the negative emotions their behaviors elicit in you are your responsibility, not theirs.

Lost in Translation

While finding the right words to express yourself is crucially important, communication is so much more than just talking. Nonverbal communication plays a vital role beyond the words you speak. Four key aspects of nonverbal communication are listening, silence, tone, and body language, so keep an eye on these:

> **Listen as much as you speak.** We talked about the importance of listening in the chapter on curiosity, but listening also plays an integral part in effective communication. It often takes a back seat, overshadowed by an eagerness to talk, but listening communicates so much—it shows the other person that you're present, that you care what they have to say, and that you want to collaborate. Active listening involves not just hearing the words but truly processing their meaning, tone, and context, and it enables you to react more accurately to what a person is thinking, feeling, wanting, and needing. The importance of listening is central to my work, and despite having spent almost two decades listening professionally, I know it's a skill I will always be working to improve.

It can be hard to know when to speak and when to listen—when in doubt about what someone needs, just ask! When someone comes to you with a problem, you can ask them, "Do you want solutions, or do you want empathy?" Sometimes, they just want an empathetic ear. If that's the case, resist the overwhelming urge to give advice. Advice is spoken in the language of experience—if someone doesn't share your experience, it will be hard for them to relate to your advice. Similarly, when you share a problem with someone, it helps to let them know beforehand if you're hoping that they'll problem-solve with you or just listen.

Leave some room. We talked about the importance of silence with Meghan in the mindfulness chapter—Meghan's inability to tolerate silence made it tough, at times, to communicate with herself and others. Silence is not an absence of communication but a powerful tool for effective dialogue. It allows space for reflecting, processing information, and considering responses thoughtfully. You'll be amazed what people share with you when you don't jump in right away. In social interactions, strategic silence can indicate self-awareness, empathy, and respect for others' perspectives.

Watch your tone. Often, it's not what you say but *how* you say it that matters. The biggest aspect of communication to take a hit in the digital age is tone. If you've ever tried to convey sarcasm through text, you know how much can get lost when we can't hear the way someone is saying something. What may sound thoughtful in your head can come across as controlling, a joke may be read as cutting, nonchalance may be misconstrued as disinterest. Before you hit send, imagine being the receiver of your message (and for an extra tool to help with this, read about how to utilize "remojis" later in the chapter).

Show don't tell. A study by Nalini Ambady and Robert Rosenthal found that students could accurately predict a teacher's effectiveness based solely on silent video clips lasting just a few seconds, demonstrating the profound impact of nonverbal behavior. Body language is a critical aspect of nonverbal communication—it conveys emotions, attitudes, and intentions through physical cues. If you're talking about being excited and present but you're hunched over and looking down with your arms crossed, you're communicating two opposing things. According to renowned anthropologist Ray Birdwhistell, approximately 65 percent of the meaning in an interaction is derived from nonverbal cues. Body language encompasses everything from facial expressions and eye contact to posture and gestures, often revealing unspoken thoughts and feelings. To learn more about your style, ask a friend or colleague if you can record your next meeting or conversation. Watch it back and pay attention to your nonverbal gestures and cues.

Conflict and Communication

As I worked with Stephanie to understand her resistance to saying no, we discovered that underneath her aversion to the word *no* lived a fear of conflict. Stephanie bent over backward to avoid conflict everywhere in her life. Annoyances with friends and loved ones would grow into frustrations, which soon became resentments, and then, eventually, explosions over the smallest issues. Stephanie kept things mostly copacetic with her colleagues, often at the expense of her own needs. But then, Kyle, an assertive (and let's be honest, a bit arrogant) man joined her team and quickly began questioning her and undermining her decisions.

Stephanie shared her frustrations with me in a session one day. "He's not a bad guy. . . . I think he's just confident and eager. But every time I share a direction we should take our campaign, he plays devil's advocate and pushes a completely different idea. Even when I suggest where we should order lunch, he jumps in with somewhere we should order from instead. I know I should set up a one-on-one with him and figure it out, but you know I hate saying no and I *really* hate conflict of any kind."

For a while, Stephanie said nothing when Kyle interrupted and contradicted her in meeting after meeting. But in avoiding a tough conversation, Stephanie was contributing to a problematic dynamic. Over time, her anger compounded. "I have actual fantasies of smothering this guy," she admitted to me in session one day with a small laugh to show me she was (mostly) joking. "I know it's ridiculous, I don't think he even *realizes* how annoyed I am with him, which just pisses me off even more."

"Well, how *would* he know if you don't show it, or better yet, say something?" I asked.

Stephanie's inertia contradicted the very persona she was trying to shed—the newbie assistant who started at the company years ago and wasn't able to stand up for herself. Her work was suffering, and her stress levels rose as she internalized the issue rather than addressing it head-on. The problem was solvable, though, if she was willing to lean toward conflict instead of away from it with Kyle.

THE BEAUTY OF CONFLICT:
FROM BREAKDOWNS TO BREAKTHROUGHS

If the thought of conflict makes you squirm, you're far from alone. Conflict is uncomfortable for most people, especially when it's with someone you love, care about, or depend on. Most people did not have healthy and thoughtful examples of conflict modeled to them growing up. Some people had parents who never fought in front of them, even when it was clear that things were "off." Other people might have witnessed a ton of conflict growing up but not a lot of conflict resolution. For all kinds of reasons, your relationship to conflict might be complicated.

But in any relationship, whether it's romantic or platonic, with family, or at work, I believe that *conflict in a relationship is like exercise to a muscle.* Think about it this way: Exercise creates microtears in muscle. When you lift weights, you are actually doing a tiny bit of damage to your muscles. If you worked that same muscle over and over and never rested, you'd permanently damage it. But, if you allow for repair by resting, drinking water, eating protein, and getting a good night's sleep, then the muscle will heal stronger than it was before and will adapt to better handle the stress of future exercise. Over time, not only will you be able to lift more weight than you could before, but you'll also be more equipped to handle other kinds of stress on your body.

This is how I think about conflict in a relationship. The key is repair. When you work through conflict thoughtfully, your relationship will be stronger and better able to handle stress than it was before. And, in fact, there's a certain type of strength and closeness that a relationship can only have on the other side of conflict. I'm sure you can think of a relationship in your life where you've gone through something tough together, but you came out the other side closer than you were before.

So how do you repair? That's where communication comes in. Repair is about circling back and talking through what happened, sharing your feelings, owning your part, and thinking together about what could be different the next time. Lean in, because any relationship that can be ruined by a thoughtful conversation about how you feel and what you need doesn't have long-term stability or potential anyway. Conflict between two people is always cocreated by both people, and each party has to explore and own up to their own contributions to the disagreement. This is hard to do if you don't trust that the other person will do the same. Ideally, both people come toward what I call "the middle of the boat" at the same time. When locked in disagreement, you may take an extreme position to counteract your partner. Each of you worries that if you lean in at all, the boat will capsize. If you notice this happening, summon some courage to step toward the middle and acknowledge how you might have contributed to the fight or problem. By saying, "Here is the role I think I played here," you will free up the other person to think about the role they might have played as well.

Communication Lifelines

Overcoming challenges and finding solutions can strengthen the bond between partners, friends, family members, and colleagues, fostering a healthier and more open relationship built on trust. Not a bad outcome for what could have been just a fight, right?

When it comes to conflict, the tools you have in your communication toolbox will change the game. The following are a few helpful tools to have at the ready.

1. "YOU VERSUS ME" INTO "US VERSUS THE PROBLEM"

Heading into a tough conversation? Get clear on your intention before saying a single word. Remember the "make a fist" activity I shared in the self-awareness chapter? This activity perfectly exemplifies how often people enter an interaction ready for a fight, or to defend themselves, even when everyone is on the same team. It is wildly common to have a "me versus you" mindset without even intending to or realizing it. In a "me versus you" mindset, an adversarial relationship is created instead of a collaborative one—the other person is seen as *the problem*. By shifting into an "us versus the problem" mindset, you'll reframe the problem as an external force that you and your counterpart face together. Suddenly, the problem is the problem, not the other person. By joining forces against a problem (instead of each other) you'll be much more likely to communicate effectively and find a solution.

For example, imagine one of your colleagues tends to leave their work to the last minute, which causes you stress because it doesn't leave you enough time to get your portion of the work done. It's tempting to approach them with a "me versus you" mindset (you and your work style are the problem), but this is likely to lead to accusations and defensiveness. Instead, think about the situation as "us versus work deadlines." Begin the conversation by expressing your shared goal of delivering high-quality work on time. Acknowledge the challenges your colleague may be facing and offer support in overcoming them. You might say, "I've noticed that we have different work styles—you do things right before the deadline, where I like to do things ahead of time. I want us to work together to find a solution that ensures our projects stay on track. What obstacles are you facing, and how can I support you in addressing them?" By approaching the issue as a shared challenge, you create an environment where your colleague will feel supported and motivated to find a solution collaboratively.

Stephanie and I practiced this mindset shift before having a conversation with Kyle. Stephanie, understandably, had a "me versus you" mindset with him—"my ideas versus yours / my authority versus yours / my desire to be respected and heard versus your desire to assert yourself and 'win.'" In preparing to have a conversation with Kyle, Stephanie shifted her mindset to "us versus this campaign" and "us versus a limited time in meetings to share ideas." By putting herself in this mindset, she was able to approach Kyle in a much less defensive way, and she noticed that their interactions became more productive and collaborative.

This tool works well in your personal life, too. Consider a situation where you and your partner have been arguing about household chores. You feel that you're taking on more than your fair share and want to confront them about it. Instead of approaching the issue as "me versus you," reframe it as "us versus the unbalanced workload." Initiate a conversation with your partner, focusing on your shared desire for a harmonious and equitable household. You could say, "We're both so busy, and there are also a lot of chores to do. I know we both want to create a home where we feel supported and appreciated. Let's think together about how we can divide tasks more fairly and find a system that works for both of us." By presenting the problem as a shared challenge, you invite your partner to collaborate and find a solution that benefits your relationship as a whole.

2. NVC IS THE MVP

In 2014, when Satya Nadella took over as CEO of Microsoft, he handed out a book at his first executive meeting called *Nonviolent*

Communication by psychologist Marshall Rosenberg. I'm sure it was met with raised eyebrows, hushed objections, and subtle smirks. At the time, it was widely known that the company was ruled by open hostility and infighting under its former CEO. Nadella knew he was walking into a minefield of toxicity, and he was determined to change that. Nadella saw how the business could work better—and be better to its employees—through nonviolent communication. In a corporate world of sharp elbows and sharp tongues, Nadella wanted to practice a kinder, gentler, more collaborative way of doing things. More than ten years later, he has been praised for reshaping the culture of the company and, by doing so, burnishing the company's then-tarnished image.

The creator of the nonviolent communication model, Dr. Rosenberg developed his ideas while working on racial integration in schools and other organizations in the South during the sixties. He wanted to show kids who had vastly different life experiences that they could still connect and work through conflict together. Nonviolent communication (also known as NVC), is based on the theory that if you can relay a problem based on your feelings and needs, then there's a much higher chance that the other party will be able to understand and empathize because they, too, have those feelings and needs at various times in their lives. Over time, Rosenberg's philosophy has proven very effective in setting up a value system that puts everyone—no matter their life experiences—on the same playing field. At its core, NVC is a conflict-resolution language. It teaches people to lower their defensiveness and it decreases misunderstandings. Underneath everything, Rosenberg explains, we all have the same feelings, and we all have the same needs.

While I won't be able to explain NVC sufficiently here (I highly recommend you pick up the book and learn about it more thoroughly), the basic principle is as follows. When working through a conflict or problematic interpersonal dynamic, you should use this template to communicate the issue:

> When I observed _____, I felt _____ because my need for _____ was not met. In the future, would you be willing to _____?

Those four fill-in-the-blanks (adult Mad Libs, if you will) represent four components to work through in any given situation. Let's use the example of a team member forgetting to follow up with an important client.

1. **Observation (*When I observed . . .*):** What did you see? What did you hear? Instead of saying, "You are so unreliable . . ." (that's a judgment, not an observation), you would say exactly what happened, "You said you were going to follow up with the client on Tuesday, but then you didn't. . . ." Avoid words like "always" and "never" in your observations (it's almost *never* true that someone *always* does anything). Just the facts.

2. **Feelings (*I felt . . .*):** How do you feel about what you observed? Don't tell them what you *thought*, tell them what you *felt*. So instead of, "I felt like you were irresponsible" (that's a thought not a feeling), you would say, "I felt frustrated and anxious."

3. **Needs (*My need for . . . was not met*):** Which of your needs are not being met as a result of this situation (Rosenberg includes a list of the "universal human needs" that you can choose from—things like safety, love, understanding, creativity, autonomy, meaning, etc.)? So in our example, you might say, "My need for support was not met."

4. **Requests (*In the future, would you be willing to . . .*):** What would you like the other person to do or say moving forward? This is not a demand (meaning that you have to accept that they may or may not honor your request). You could ask, "In the future, can you include me in your follow-up emails so I have a sense of when they've been done?"

So with NVC, instead of saying, "When you bail on clients, you're being super irresponsible. Next time you need to do what you say you're going to do," you would say, "When you didn't follow up with the client on Tuesday like you said you would, I felt frustrated because I want to feel supported on this project but ended up feeling anxious about the potential impact on our client relationship. In the future, would you be willing to CC me on your emails so I can keep track of where we are with things?"

Once you've communicated in this way, the other person ultimately gets to decide whether or not to meet your request. If they don't want to meet it, the agency is back on you to determine what to do. (Do you decide to rely on them less? Report them to management? Request to change teams?) NVC is wildly helpful in every part of life, even at home: "When you leave your dishes in the sink, I feel annoyed because collaboration is important to me. In the future, would you be willing to put your dishes away by the end of the night?" tends to go better than, "Stop leaving your f*cking dishes in the sink, you inconsiderate asshole."

Stephanie and I talked about how to use NVC language to have a conversation with Kyle. What she probably wanted to say was, "Hey, Kyle, you're super arrogant and annoying. Stop picking apart and one-upping every idea I have." If she said that to Kyle, he'd probably get defensive and the conversation would go nowhere fast. But here's nonviolent communication to the rescue:

Observation: "Hey, Kyle, I noticed in our last team meeting that you spoke over me and shared reasons why my idea wouldn't work before I finished explaining it."

Feelings: "When this happened, I felt irritated and dejected."

Needs: "To do great work together, I need to feel like we're collaborating and on the same team."

Request: "In future meetings, would you be up for trying to build on the things I share before shooting them down? I bet together we could come up with some really great ideas."

When Stephanie expressed this to Kyle, he was shocked. He didn't even realize that he'd come across as shooting down Stephanie's ideas, and they talked about what having a more collaborative and playful relationship might look like.

3. SWAP POSITIONS

Have you ever wished you could swap lives with someone? Maybe you'd love to be a celebrity or athlete for a day. There is something so enticing about seeing the world through another person's eyes, and yet, we often neglect to do it when we need to the most. When it comes to handling a disagreement—when you and a conflict partner can't seem to come to a decision, swapping positions can be a very effective tool. This works great for cofounders, colleagues, romantic partners, friends—really any two people at an impasse.

The way this works is that any time you and your partner, colleague, or friend disagree about something and can't come to a decision, have the discussion again, but swap positions—now you each have to argue the other person's side of the disagreement. This works because:

1. It loosens everyone's attachment to being "right" because now you each have a horse in both races.

2. It helps you see each other's perspective.

3. You may generate new ideas that the other person hadn't even thought of, which might make the best choice more clear.

The next time Kyle played devil's advocate with one of Stephanie's ideas, she used this tool to introduce a more playful approach. Here's how that went:

Stephanie: I have an idea for this new campaign. I think we should focus on the idea of "natural beauty," highlighting how this brand enhances a person's natural features. We can use models with minimal makeup to showcase how the products bring out their best selves. This will appeal to customers who want a more natural look. . . .

Kyle: Eh, that won't work. This brand is known for luxury and glamour . . . customers expect a certain level of sophistication. A natural look will seem too casual.

Stephanie: Okay, Kyle I get it . . . but are you up for a little game? Let's swap positions—I have to think of reasons why a natural-beauty campaign isn't the way to go, you have to think of reasons why it is.

Kyle: Okay, you're on. So . . . a natural beauty campaign could work if we position it as a way to show how these products are so high-quality that you don't need a lot of makeup to look amazing. We could use models with different skin tones and features to showcase that luxury works for everyone. And we could emphasize the idea of "effortless beauty"—like you woke up looking this good.

Stephanie: I love that! Okay, my turn. So I see what you mean about staying true to the brand's image. We don't want to lose the luxury and glamour that our customers expect. What if we did a campaign that shows how our products can transform your look from day to night? We could show a model going from a natural daytime look to a more glamorous evening look, all using our products. We'll showcase the versatility of the brand and appeal to customers who want both natural and sophisticated options.

Kyle: Oh, I actually love that! We could even do a series of looks for different occasions—work, weekend, special events, etc. That way, we show how our products fit into every aspect of our customers' lives. Maybe we even use language like "elevate your natural beauty" as a nod to the combo of natural and glamour.

By swapping positions, Stephanie and Kyle were able to see each other's perspectives, generate new ideas, and find a solution that satisfied both of their concerns. In the end, they came up with a winning campaign concept that stayed true to their brand while also appealing to a wider range of customers.

4. PERSPECTIVE SHIFTING

Do you have a friend, partner, or colleague who is, for better or worse, just different than you are? Where you're anxious, they're laid-back.

Where you're up for anything, they're particular. Maybe they're so organized they'd put Marie Kondo to shame but you like to follow a plan naturally as it unfolds. To better communicate with someone who is wired differently than you are, try putting things into their perspective, on their terms. For example, my best friend and I are very different people in many ways: I'm an extrovert, she's an introvert. She loves canceled plans and hates surprises. I love surprises and want to be social as often as possible. For the most part, we balance each other out nicely, but sometimes our differences make it tough to naturally empathize and communicate with each other.

Many years ago, she canceled plans on me at the last minute (something she did often), and I got upset. She couldn't understand why—wasn't I relieved to have the night to myself? I tried to explain it to her in her own language: "When you cancel our plans at the last minute, it makes me feel the way I imagine *you* would feel if I invited a bunch of people to our dinner date without checking in with you." Ah, she got it: "My bad. I thought I was doing you a favor, but it sounds like, really, you felt like I didn't consider you," she reflected back to me. That was exactly it. Same feelings but different perspectives. By giving her a scenario she could understand, I helped her feel what I was feeling (thank you, empathy). Of course, this tool requires not only self-awareness but also deep empathy and understanding of the other person's operating system.

5. COMPLAIN WITHOUT BLAME

Add this question to your communication repertoire: "Can I complain without blame?" This phrase will come in handy when you want to voice a frustration to someone without implying it's their fault. It's a way to go from "me versus you" to "us versus the problem" and prevent the other person from feeling blamed or getting defensive.

Example:

😊: Can I complain without blame for a sec?
🙂: Sure, what's up?
😊: We're way over budget this month.
🙂: Hmm . . . how can we work together to spend less?

Or:

😊: Hey, I want to complain without blame about something.
🙂: Okay, what's going on?
😊: We don't go out much these days. We used to do all kinds of exciting things together.
🙂: Yeah, we've been on the couch a lot . . . should we plan a fun night out?

Hint: This phrase only works if you don't follow it with something blaming. You can't say, "Can I complain without blame? You're terrible at your job!" Use it for collaboration and growth.

The Proactive Approach

Of course, a proactive approach to communication is ideal. If you can prevent small problems from becoming big problems, you'll be saving yourself a lot of time and strife. First and foremost, it's important to be transparent, direct, and a bit vulnerable with your communication. And timing is everything. If you have something to say that will be tough to hear, you want whoever is hearing it to be in the right frame of mind. Make sure they're not running off to a meeting or under a deadline. Check in by setting the scene: "Do you have the space right now to talk through an issue I've been having? It might be heavy. If now's not a great time, I can put something on your calendar for later today."

By practicing communicating in lower-stakes situations, you'll be that much more prepped when a bigger issue does come up, and you'll already have the tools to work through it. Here are two helpful tools for communicating proactively:

RELATIONSHIP RETRO

Institute a "relationship retro" with those you interact with most. Once a week, month, or quarter, schedule a planned sit-down with any important colleague, partner, roommate, family member, or friend in your life. During this meetup, you'll each answer these questions:

During the past week / month / quarter . . .

1. I appreciated / you showed up for me / I felt understood when . . .

2. I felt dropped / I found myself worrying / I felt frustrated when . . .

3. One way we can support each other next week / month / quarter is . . .

By doing this proactively and regularly, you'll create a safe space where each person can practice voicing their needs and being heard, and you'll both flex your communication muscle in the process.

GET VISUAL: REMOJIS

Since technology has made communicating exponentially faster and efficient, you'd think it would have gotten more effective, too. When it comes to communicating emotional information, though, a lot is lost through text (has autocorrect ever actually corrected anything accurately?). Still, texts, emails, and Slacks are here to stay, so we need a better way to make sure we're getting our thoughts across clearly. An unconventional solution is built right in: the emoji. My use of emojis went way up because of a friend who was much more visual in his thinking, and I realized how powerful these tiny icons can be to convey complicated information. For example, look at the difference between these two messages:

🧑: I can't believe you did that

😊: Omg I'm sorry, I didn't mean to upset you!

versus

🧑: I can't believe you did that 😂

😊: I know, right? It was hilarious!

The only difference between the two messages is one emoji. They're instant and intuitive game changers.

By proactively assigning an emoji to a piece of information that you're trying to communicate, you can save yourself—and your fellow texting recipients—from awkward and confusing exchanges. I call these types of emojis "remojis" (I just squished the words *remote* and *emojis* together), and I use these at work, as well as with my family and friends. At Coa, whenever there's some kind of miscommunication via text, we assign a remoji to prevent it from happening again. For example, we use an upside-down face emoji 🙃 to imply sarcasm (because we all know humor can get lost easily through text). A heart with a bandage 💗 means *I'm feeling a little sensitive today, so maybe it's not the best day to give me negative feedback or to be really hard on me.* I use these with friends, too. A few include: 😣 😷, which means *I had a bad day but don't want to talk about it,* 👀💘 means *the message you just sent is ridiculous but I love you anyway,* and 🔲 means *I'm putting my phone down now.* A picture is worth a thousand words, right?

Another helpful remoji to enter the chat: I noticed that when my cofounder and I would text each other about problems at the company, neither of us would know if the other person was *upset* about the problem, or if they just wanted help *solving* the problem. In those moments, it was hard to know if we should tend to the problem or the relationship. We decided to use the chili pepper emoji 🌶 if we're upset. So if there's a pepper at the end of a message, it means *I'm feeling spicy about this problem.* With no chili pepper, it just means *please help me with the problem.*

Remojis might seem a little silly, but the sheer number of problems prevented, crises averted, and negative feelings avoided proves their power. As with any language, it may feel a little contrived at first, but in time, it will feel automatic on both sides of the screen. Here are a few examples of remojis:

🙌 = I got your back, you're awesome, go us

🕐 = I see this message and will get back to you later

🙃 = Said with sarcasm

🧠 = Let's think before we take action

💗 = I'm feeling sensitive today

◔ = We can move on, but I'd like to circle back about this

☀ = This is urgent, and I need a response ASAP

☺ = This is not urgent; take your time

🙇 = I'm heads down today

🌙 = I'm upset about this situation

Where in your life could remojis improve your communication? For the next week, track anything you've said through text that landed flat or created a misunderstanding. At the end of the week, review the list. Is there a remoji you could suggest that would prevent the same issue in the future? Make a list of remojis to share at work and at home. Make it fun! Remojis will become a private language that you speak with people. You'll be surprised how quickly people lean in.

Boundaried Vulnerability

The question I get most often about communicating is: *How much* should people communicate about themselves, especially at work? Is it possible to be honest and open, while still keeping it professional? To find the right balance here, I like to talk about "boundaried vulnerability," which is the balancing act of sharing enough of yourself that you invite connection with others without sharing so much that you ask your colleagues to become your therapist. When it comes to sharing about ourselves at work, we all tend to be somewhere on a spectrum from "too tight" to "too leaky." Imagine you have a meeting with your manager and they show up looking really flustered or overwhelmed. You ask if they're okay . . .

Someone who is too leaky may respond this way: "No, actually. I am about to have a nervous breakdown. Peter up in accounting has been on my case all week about that budget, but I can't seem to finish it. I'm having problems at home, and my wife is about to divorce me. Seriously, she's not even talking to me. I'm a mess over it—I can't work, I can't eat, I can't sleep. . . . What should I do?"

Yikes, right? They've become a puddle on the floor that you now need to clean up. When someone is too leaky, they overshare and rely on others to be their therapists. And it puts the other person in an awkward position to try to care for them in ways that they are not equipped to handle nor responsible for.

On the other hand, the manager who is too tight might say: "I'm completely fine . . . everything is great." This response is too buttoned-up and doesn't show *any* vulnerability, which in turn closes down any connection from others. Usually, people can tell when something is wrong, so a "too tight" response can feel inauthentic. I'm sure you know people like this—people you've worked with for years but barely know a thing about.

The sweet spot is in the middle of this spectrum. This is where boundaried vulnerability exists. It's more of an art than a science, and how much you should share will be context dependent. It will depend on who you're talking to and what environment you're in. Taking the example from above, a person with boundaried vulnerability would respond this way: "Thanks for asking. I'm having a tough day, there's a lot going on that I'm sorting through. I've been navigating some personal issues, but I'm getting the support I need. I appreciate you checking in."

So, how do you identify if something you want to share is going to be too tight or too leaky? Ask yourself three questions: (1) If the person I share this with responds with a nod and quickly moves on from the discussion, would I be okay with that or would I regret sharing? (2) Is this the best person to share this information with? Or would it be better suited for my best friend, my therapist, or my partner? (3) Would sharing this allow me to show up as a whole human without asking anyone to fix my problems or take care of me? A lot of self-awareness and empathy goes into answering these three questions, so make sure you flex these muscles while working through such a scenario.

––––––

Stephanie leaned into all of these communication tools to shift the way she expressed herself with Kyle. She had to accept that some conflict might be necessary to get to a better and stronger place and accept that things might feel a bit worse between them before they felt better. By confronting her frustration head-on, owning and voicing her needs, and getting a little playful (more on that in the next chapter), Stephanie and Kyle were able to create a collaborative relationship that eventually became an authentic friendship.

Ultimately, Stephanie learned to navigate confrontation more effectively. She learned to tune into her true feelings, establish appropriate boundaries, and better communicate those boundaries to others. As a result, she saw rapid improvement across the board in her personal and professional relationships. Since she no longer walked around feeling abused and exploited, her feelings of resentment and alienation abated.

Communication Push-up: Express Yourself

Now it's your turn—time for some communication crunches. This push-up is for anyone who has ever minimized a need or desire in their life, or hoped that someone would "just know" what that need or desire is.

STEP 1: Think of one thing that you've been hoping your colleague, boss, friend, or significant other would do or say that you've never explicitly asked for. Maybe you wish they would do a better job recognizing your work, or perhaps you wish they would call you more. Maybe you wish they would be more specific with their feedback, or you wish they would spend more time with your family.

STEP 2: Write down how you might ask for this person to meet your need. You can try using this NVC-adjacent template: "I'm working on asking for what I need more directly instead of assuming that you know. I've realized that I really wish you would . . . X. But I've never told you! This is important to me because . . . Y. Is this something you might be willing to do?" Take a second to imagine if someone made this ask of you. Does it feel reasonable? Specific? Doable? Think about how it'll feel if they then meet that need, and how it'll feel if they decide not to.

STEP 3: The final step of this push-up is to actually make the ask! Of course, the person might say no. Or they might say yes and then not do it. These are the realities of relationship life. But you will at least have owned and communicated your need, which is most important.

Now that you have flexed your way through this communication circuit, you have one more trait to go. Ready to get to that finish line? Good, because after all this hard work, I think it's time to **play**.

9 PLAYFULNESS

Saying "Yes, and . . ."

Play is the answer to the question: how does
anything new come about?

—JEAN PIAGET

"Maybe instead of focusing on making little jokes, she should focus on making the company some money. Honestly, I'm done with her. You're either with me or you're against me. That's it."

My client, Angelo, a technology strategist at a top-tier financial firm, was telling me about a colleague who had poked fun at him in a meeting for being "too serious." I'd been working with Angelo for a few months, and I was very fond of him. But I didn't disagree with his colleague. Left-brain-oriented, Angelo was logical, direct, and a rule-keeper, and he had trouble stepping out of his linear way of thinking. He ran a tight ship at work—meetings were always on time and on point. He took his job and himself very seriously, and he expected the same of everyone around him. His efficiency would be envied by any military commander, but his impervious, rigid ways left little room for his team to think organically or brainstorm ideas.

Equally rigid in his personal life, Angelo wrote people off left and right the moment they pissed him off. He had fallen out with several friends over the years due to minor disagreements that he blew out of proportion. In Angelo's mind, there was no room for nuance or different perspectives. If a friend challenged one of his strongly held views, even in a respectful way, he would take it as a personal betrayal. He couldn't grasp that two people could have differing opinions yet still respect and care for each other. This black-or-white thinking extended to his romantic life as well. Every person Angelo dated was "the one" until he caught a glimpse of any imperfection, then they were history. All of his relationships were strained as he struggled to appreciate each person as a whole—flaws and all. In other words, at work and at home, there was no room for play.

Tricks Are Not Just for Kids

What comes to mind when you think about the word *play*? Images of kids running around playgrounds or pretending in make-believe scenarios? Our society tends to associate play solely with children, and as those children grow older and become adults, they may view play as an unproductive or unnecessary part of everyday life. Who has time in their overscheduled, overcaffeinated, overstressed lives for play, anyway? In a results-driven corporate world, the upside of play can be difficult to perceive through a narrow lens.

But what does it really mean to play and be playful? At its core, our seventh and final trait of playfulness is the ability to imaginatively explore the realm of what's possible in any situation without attachment to specific outcomes. Everything—I mean everything—that has ever been created in this world has come about as a result of play. Play is serious stuff. For driven souls and type A personalities, play may serve the purpose of competition. But in relation to emotional health, play is not about results or winning. Although structured games with rigid rules and scoreboards are forms of play, play in its purest form is an unbounded, free-flowing experimentation. With play, the means is more important than the end. And the very act of being playful opens up a world of possibilities, which is crucial in any work or home environment. Rather than distracting you, playfulness can ignite you.

As psychologist Michael Parsons puts it, "Play functions to sustain a paradoxical reality where things can be real and not real at the same time." In his influential paper discussing the importance of play in therapy, Parsons uses karate as a metaphor. "Karate training is not a real fight. But although we were only pretending to fight, we had to pretend seriously. Knowing that we were not engaged in a real fight allowed us to make our attacks with full seriousness and commitment, to make them as real as we possibly could."

In other words, play creates an "as if" quality. It's a chance to try things on as if they're real but without the same risk as if they were actually happening. This as-if mentality is arguably the seedbed of creativity itself. It allows you to envision and inhabit alternate realities, breaking free of constraints to prototype new ideas. It's like a rehearsal space where you can improvise before stepping onto the grander stage of real-life implementations and consequences.

Look around. Most likely, you're already engaging in play in this way at work and at home. Whether you're interviewing for a job or going on a first date, you're playing. In both cases, you engage in as-if scenarios: you're not yet in a relationship, nor are you working together yet. But in a way that is both real and not real at the same time, you're playacting that you are. You're trying each other on and sussing out what it might *feel* like to be or work together. A start-up is basically a concretized version of this—it's as if a company has launched, before it actually has. Play can also be as simple as having a "no bad ideas in a brainstorm" session, or letting your mind wander to what you would do if you won the lottery. In all of these scenarios, you are being playful.

In the workplace, we've seen many tech companies embrace the idea of playfulness: from Ping-Pong tables in the office to icebreaker games at the beginning of video calls, playfulness at work will boost creativity (and therefore productivity), deepen community (fewer office politics), and increase overall job satisfaction (and thus lower turnover). Tech isn't the only industry to embrace play: creative fields like media and gaming have been integrating play in their workspaces as well, and as more information comes out about how critical play is for emotional health, more and more industries are embracing its power. Hugely successful TV producer Shonda Rhimes championed the use of playfulness in her production company, Shondaland, to create an environment that fostered collaboration and creativity. The writers for *Grey's Anatomy*, for instance, would engage in paint-by-numbers, create Play-Doh sculptures, or work on puzzles as they worked to create fresh storylines.

Ultimately, being playful is about granting yourself the permission to think divergently, try on new perspectives, and fail without catastrophic consequences. It paradoxically engages you more fully in the present moment while expanding your capacity to envision alternative futures. Play may be one of the most undervalued tools for navigating the complexities of our modern world. As we'll explore in the following sections, nurturing a playful spirit can catalyze creativity, resilience, and emotional well-being across all facets of your life.

It Pays to Play

Playing is fundamental to the human experience. It allows you to purposefully disengage from the stresses of daily life in order to re-engage with a refreshed, more vibrant spirit. It fosters deeper connections and stronger bonds whether you're playing with family, friends, or coworkers. While some may dismiss play as a "nice to have" instead of a "must have," a growing body of scientific evidence reveals its critical role in our social, cognitive, emotional, and even physical development across the entire lifespan. For example, evolutionary psychologists like Peter Gray of Boston College posit that for our earliest ancestors, childhood play laid the foundations for developing vital cooperative and sharing skills that enabled survival into adulthood.

A wealth of research supports how play influences emotional well-being across all ages. In their seminal work on play theory, psychologists Brian Sutton-Smith and Diana Kelly-Byrne synthesized decades of studies showing how play shapes everything from cognitive abilities to social skills to emotional resilience. Far from mere frivolity, being playful allows us to safely experiment, take risks, and push boundaries in ways that foster flexible thinking, problem-solving, and innovation. This dynamic is beautifully illustrated in the play rituals of many social animals. Dogs extend "play bows" to initiate romping sessions with one another. Birds like ravens and crows engage in vocal mimicry games. Otters joyfully slide down muddy hills. Even bees have been observed nonchalantly batting around small balls in midair. Across species, play seems to serve as a kind of social glue, forging trust and camaraderie within groups. Play is a vital part of the social contract of any intelligent animal.

Today, play is just as important to help children develop a host of skills from socialization to self-regulation, and it creates the safe space all kids need for stable relationships. Playful kids learn more quickly and retain more of what they learn by their own innate curiosity. It gives them a sense of independence and confidence, and if play is physical, improves overall physical health. Pioneering psychoanalyst Donald Winnicott, who studied play's profound importance, eloquently captured this symbiotic relationship: "It is only in playing that the individual is able to be creative and to use the whole personality, and it is only in being creative that the individual discovers the self."

On the flip side, a lack of opportunities for childhood play has been associated with increased risks of antisocial behavior later in life. Pioneering researcher Stuart Brown, founder and president of the National Institute for Play, interviewed thousands of individuals, including incarcerated youth, over many years. He found a striking correlation between childhoods bereft of play with tendencies toward criminal activities and violence as adults. While the causes of such behaviors are multifaceted, these findings hint at play's profound role in healthy psychosocial development and socialization from an early age.

Play's benefits for mental health extend far beyond childhood, too. Sutton-Smith boldly declared that the opposite of play is not work, it's depression. Play provides a crucial pressure valve to cope with prolonged uncertainty and emotional burdens during crisis periods. It can be therapeutic, calming nerves and diffusing stress. In certain cases, engaging in playful activities has been shown to alleviate anxiety, depression, and other mental health challenges more effectively than some pharmaceutical treatments. For example, one study showed how playing online games can outperform pharma in treating anxiety and depression—assuming participants do not indulge in too much screen time.

And when it comes to being playful, you should play the long game. Seniors playing chess in parks are on to something, and as you grow older, the importance of play remains a constant: research shows that adults who play regularly are happier and more creative. While many factors influence long-term health, play can improve cognitive functioning and memory, physical and emotional health, and even longevity. Laughter, often a product of play, has been shown to help your clock keep ticking for longer, and one study has shown that humor can add on eight years to your life. It's no laughing matter that the more playful you are, the longer and better you will live. After all, we don't stop playing because we grow old, we grow old because we stop playing.

Of course, like anything else, technology is changing what it means to play as we increasingly shift our daily interactions from face-to-face to screen-to-screen. And while the virtual and digital world that we now live in has made certain types of communication and connection more possible, it is hobbling the opportunity for play for children and adults alike. Even as you're constantly in contact with other people on Slack, email, and text—it's unlikely that you'll be playful in the same way in those mediums as you would be in person. I've had a lot of clients talk about how, despite enjoying remote work, they miss the serendipitous, playful office interactions they used to have. We need to play more than ever, and while it's more difficult to engage digitally, it's still possible.

Play It Safe

Have I convinced you that playing is not just for kids? Good, because while play is indeed fun and joyful, reclaiming your playful spirit as an adult can be surprisingly tricky. When I was first examining the seven traits of emotional fitness, I wondered if playfulness should be first, because being playful will help you lower your defenses (curiosity), connect with others (empathy), and get through difficult moments (resilience). But to truly play, you must have at least begun to hone all of these skills. The stronger your mindfulness, curiosity, self-awareness, resilience, empathy, and communication, the more playful you'll naturally become, and in the end, the ability to play is a sign that you have been doing your reps. Of course, the more playful you are, the more you'll strengthen these other traits as well.

So why don't we play more? Many dismiss the importance of being playful because they don't believe they have the time for it or don't think it's a top priority in their lives. But living underneath these excuses is a more complicated truth: to truly play is to be vulnerable. When you play, your guard will come down naturally, and that can be scary if you're a person who works hard to keep your guard up. Your worries about play might look like a lack of confidence in how to play (*I'm not good at it*), a worry about rejection (*What if I put myself out there and no one joins in?*), or a concern about other's perception of you (*People will think I'm unprofessional*). Not only does playing with others mean risking feelings of being abandoned in a vulnerable space (if you've ever made a joke that's fallen flat and received only blank or judgmental stares, you know how terrible this can feel), but playing also means peeking into hidden parts of yourself (hello, self-awareness), which can be scary if you're not sure what you'll find.

Having done years of play therapy with kids and playful talk therapy with adults, I can tell you that people only play freely when they feel safe. Play requires a deep sense of trust in the process and in the people you're playing with. Play is both seriously important and seriously difficult, because stepping into a world of "what if" means leaning into the unknown (hey there, mindfulness). It means being willing to start something without knowing exactly where it will finish. If you're not in a safe space for vulnerability, you will not lean into play. To be playful, you'll need to be okay with feeling untethered and have some assurance that while you don't actually know where you're going, you're going to get somewhere important.

This makes playfulness especially important in leadership. Playful leaders create space for new perspectives and can meet the creativity of a team with openness. If a leader's playfulness muscle is weak, they will come off as rigid, regimented, and closed-minded (like Angelo). This tendency to shut down play without meaning to can damage relationships and sap leadership potential. In a crisis, they'll find themself doubling down on control at the very moment when flexibility and originality become most valuable. And unless leadership shows that it is safe and acceptable to be playful, no one else will feel truly safe to play either.

A Safe Space

You've likely heard the term *psychological safety* at one time or another. It's an environment in which people trust that they can express ideas, ask questions, raise concerns, or make mistakes without fear of negative consequences, such as punishment, humiliation, or rejection. When individuals feel psychologically safe, they are more likely to take risks, be creative, and collaborate effectively with others—in other words, they're more likely to play.

The importance of psychological safety was highlighted in a groundbreaking study conducted by Google, known as Project Aristotle. The study, which analyzed data from over 180 teams across the company, sought to identify the key factors that contribute to successful team performance. Surprisingly, the researchers found that the most critical factor was not the individual talents or expertise of team members, but rather the presence of psychological safety within the group. Teams with high levels of psychological safety consistently outperformed those lacking this essential element, demonstrating better problem-solving abilities, increased innovation, and higher overall productivity.

Whether at work or at home, creating a space of psychological safety is the first step in enabling yourself and those around you to be playful. When enough safety is created that people can play, an incredible cycle is kick-started. Because being playful with others also *creates* feelings of psychological safety. Putting yourself out there and being truly met in that space by those around you is a life hack for deepening connection. Think about the last time you made a silly joke to a stranger, and instead of calling you out, they jumped in and kept the joke going. By being playful, you can establish the psychological safety that allows everyone around you to relax, lean into their creativity, connect with each other, and flourish.

How to Bring Your A Game

You might be wondering how it felt to do therapy with someone like Angelo. I can tell you, it was a challenge at first. When I offered alternate points of view, he grew frustrated. When I couldn't give him clarity, I was a "crappy therapist." But to his credit, he showed up week after week. And I knew that he was in the right place, because at its core, therapy is a space where clients learn *how* to play. It's a collaborative process of what-if scenarios. The therapeutic relationship between myself and the client becomes a microcosm for the rest of their life, a safe space where they can experiment with different ideas and approaches without the fear of consequences. And the therapy room becomes a laboratory where they can try on different roles and rehearse new strategies before implementing them in the real world. In learning to play, clients learn to approach life with a sense of wonder and curiosity, recognizing that there are multiple paths to personal growth and fulfillment.

So, how can you develop this powerhouse trait? While it can be hard to get started if you're not used to playing, I'd venture to say that it's one of the more enjoyable traits to cultivate. Let's talk about how to add some important tools to your, ahem, toybox.

LOOK INWARD

The first step to becoming a more playful person is to examine your own relationship with play. What role did play and playfulness have in your life growing up? Were you encouraged to play? Was winning the most important thing? Were there people available and excited to play with you? What is your relationship to play now? Does it have an active place in your life? Can you enjoy playing if there is no competition involved or if there is but you're not in the lead? Does the idea of playing more make you feel excited, uncomfortable, or both? Take a moment now to reflect on these questions, and pay attention to the emotions that arise in you as you think about it.

As I got to know Angelo better, the origin of his rigid ways came into view. Raised in a strict and religious household, Angelo was sent to an all-boys boarding school at the young age of six. In this environment, beds had to be made to the highest of standards. Students were not to speak unless spoken to. Punishment for disobedience was harsh. Order reigned supreme and academic rigor was prized above all else. This upbringing, while beneficial in creating a sense of regulation and routine, left little room for creativity and play.

"I've been hit with a ruler more times than I can count, but I learned the importance of discipline and achievement from an early age, and I'm proud of where it's gotten me," he told me when I asked about his experience at school.

"That makes sense, discipline is an important skill. It sounds like you got a really solid education. But what about sports? Or recess? Or even just joking around? What was your experience like in that sense?"

"Oh, there was none of that. Once, I got punished just for whistling a song out loud."

No wonder Angelo didn't feel safe to play. This understanding was a first step—I gently suggested to him that children should have space to play, and that he might have an opportunity to lean into play now in a way he wasn't able to then.

FIND THE GRAY

I'm sure at some point in your life, you've been told that things are not as black-or-white as you're painting them out to be. Through the research I conducted for these seven traits of emotional fitness and through my nearly two decades of being a therapist, I've come to understand that one of the most important hallmarks of strong mental and emotional health is the ability to exist in the gray.

Analytic psychology (the type of psychology I practice) outlines a type of emotional development that is characterized by a person's ability not to think in extremes—to accept the fact that nothing and no one is all good or all bad. This is actually quite difficult, and holding good and bad at the same time is tough for everyone. Life would be much more straightforward and simple if we could locate the good in one place and move toward it, and locate the bad in another place and move away from it. But the difficult truth is, goodness and badness exist within each of us and in everything and everyone around us (check out the ending of Pixar's *Inside Out 2* to see this concept brought to life perfectly).

This tendency to think in extremes can show up in all kinds of ways. One version of this is all-or-nothing thinking. Imagine you're trying to eat healthier but end up eating something unhealthy one day. Rather than thinking, *It's okay, I'll make healthier choices tomorrow*, you might think to yourself, *Oh well, that's all gone to hell, I might as well eat whatever I want now.* I see this show up in my life when it comes to keeping my home clean. It's either the cleanest space you've ever seen, or it's a complete and utter mess. But this polarity can be detrimental to your well-being. So why am I talking about all of this? I'm sharing this important concept because black-or-white thinking is, essentially, an inability to be playful. To play with an idea is to venture into the gray.

To practice moving away from a black-or-white mindset, do this exercise. First reflect on one place in your life where you've been using this kind of extreme thinking. Maybe it's an all-or-nothing commitment to a good habit, or a tendency to see people as all good or all bad. Perfectionism is an example of this type of thinking (it's either perfect or it's useless). So is telling your partner that they "always" or "never" do things.

Next, identify what it would look like in your example to take a few steps toward the gray. For example, I might practice tidying my space lightly rather than waiting until it's so bad that I can barely stand it and then doing an insane top-to-bottom clean. Perfectionists, maybe one step toward the gray is doing something you know you won't be able to do perfectly—maybe you even submit a report with a typo (okay, I'd have trouble with that one, too). Or the next time you catch yourself telling your partner that they "*always* prioritize their work over everything else" or "*never* clean up around the house," stop yourself and say, "Actually, that's not fair of me, it's not always/never. Let me try again to explain how I'm feeling." Then try again.

Finally, reflect on how it felt to take that step. When I practiced this by lightly tidying, it felt uncomfortable and unsatisfying. But when I got home later, it was nice that my place wasn't such a mess. By taking steps toward the gray, you will create a more realistic perspective on the world.

NO BUTS ABOUT IT

When I ask people to tell me about the last time they played, they'll generally mention a board game, a video game, or maybe a sports game. And don't get me wrong, these are all wonderful types of play. But when it comes to being playful in everyday life, I like to take a page from the world of improv, a comedic art that uses playfulness between people to create unplanned, spontaneous, and often hilarious moments of creativity and entertainment. In improv, when someone comes to you with an idea, you don't say "No." You don't say "Yes, but . . ." In fact, you don't even just say "Yes." Instead, you wholeheartedly say "Yes, and . . ." You meet this person in their idea, you build on their idea, and together, the two of you get somewhere that neither of you could have gotten alone.

There are many "no" people in the world, and plenty of "yes, but" people. When I take stock of my favorite people in life—the ones I most enjoy spending time with, the ones who make me feel like I can show up exactly as I am, the ones I love working with every single day—they all have one thing in common: they are "yes, and . . ." people. These are the people who take jokes way too far with me, who say yes to invitations knowing that whatever we get into we'll have a great time, and who support me being my true, eccentric self. When someone says something a little awkward, these are the people who jump in with their own awkwardness to turn an uncomfortable situation into a humorous one. If you've ever been supported (re: played with) in this way, you know how powerful and comforting it can be.

I remember an interaction I had with two different people a number of years ago. I had the idea to start a psychology-themed restaurant. I mentioned this to two psychologist friends. One of them said, "That's cool! But restaurants are so expensive to run." And that was it. He seemed to like my idea, but he gave me a distinctly "yes, but" response. And that was . . . fine. But then, I mentioned it to another friend. When I said that I wanted to start a psychology-themed restaurant, this friend said, "Oh my gosh, YES! And it could have explanations on the back of the menu about important psychological concepts." I *loved* this idea, and said, "Yes! And the food could have punny names, like Kentucky Freud Chicken." We went back and forth like that for a while, and not only was it a supremely fun and validating conversation, it also bonded me and my friend, and we thought of some seriously clever psychology-themed food ideas (ahem, the Oedipus plate would serve chicken *with* an egg, the Rorschach dish would be squid ink pasta).

This "yes, and . . ." attitude is as important in the workplace as it is at home. There's a reason that large companies bring in improvisers to teach leaders how to say "Yes, and . . ." This mindset will prevent you from stifling collaboration and imagination, two of the most important factors for creating new things. The simple but profound flip from "yes, but" to "yes, and" transforms every interaction. If you can't stay open to new ideas and experiences, you trap yourself in a small, confined world. But if you are open to "and," you will foster innovation and collaboration. You will meet someone where they are and move forward together, and you will find things you didn't know you were looking for. The "yes, and" boss is the one that lets you show up and try things, explores with you, and celebrates the journey as much as the destination.

A great example of this is the creation of Apple's computer mouse. When Steve Jobs approached the design firm IDEO to help create a navigational tool for the first Macintosh computer, his initial prototype resembled a boxy, joystick-like device. Instead of dismissing this idea outright (can you imagine saying no to Steve Jobs?), the IDEO team applied "yes, and . . ." thinking and got to work. They experimented with different materials, shapes, and functionalities, eventually arriving at the iconic design of the Apple mouse with its sleek, ergonomic form.

To strengthen this trait of emotional fitness, work on becoming a "yes, and . . ." person. To flex this muscle, I want you to try the "yes, and . . ." mindset challenge: Throughout your day, pay attention to moments when you can "yes, and . . ." those around you. When someone shares an idea or suggestion, respond with "Yes, and . . ." and build on their contribution. Practice suspending judgment and embracing the possibilities presented by others. Notice if you get caught up in the end goal instead of enjoying the journey to get there. Get creative with it! Whether you're brainstorming with colleagues or planning a weekend activity with friends, approach the interaction with openness and playfulness. Reflect on your experiences at the end of the day. Notice how "yes, and-ing" enhanced creativity and enjoyment in various aspects of your life.

GAMIFY YOUR LIFE

The best way to become more playful is, well . . . to play! Gamify your life by applying game-design elements and principles to everyday tasks, activities, and interactions. You'll instantly make them more engaging, motivating, and enjoyable. Here are some examples of how you can get your game on:

- On a first date? Ugh, I hate small talk, too. But a great ice-breaker question can shift interactions from surface-level niceties to connection-building exploration. Get creative with your questions instead of going with the standard "What do you do?" (Check out the list at the end of this chapter for ideas).

- Eating at a diner? Play tic-tac-toe on your paper menu with your lunch companions.

- Sitting at the park with a friend? Create a story together about the people you see around you. (Example: "I think those two people over there are on a third date and they're not sure if they like each other, but they were introduced by a mutual friend so they're really giving it a shot. . . .")

- Waiting in a long line with a friend? Play "Would you rather . . . ?" with each other.

- Need to get household chores done? Make a game out of it— see who can fold laundry the fastest or turn vacuuming into a dance contest.

There are also endless opportunities to incorporate more play in a work setting. Here are a few ways to inject and encourage playfulness at work:

- Start your meetings with an icebreaker question or game to get creative juices flowing. This sets a tone of play and connection from minute one. See the end of this chapter for examples.

- Encourage your team to approach brainstorming sessions with a playful mindset. Emphasize the "yes, and . . ." approach to build on each other's ideas. Provide paper and pens and let people know that they can doodle if that helps their creative process.

- Turn mundane tasks or projects into playful challenges. Create friendly competitions or leaderboards to motivate people and add an element of fun to goal-setting. Use rewards and incentives to encourage participation and achievement.

- Organize team-building activities that promote playfulness and foster connections among team members. Consider outdoor activities, escape rooms, or improv workshops to break down barriers and build camaraderie. I recommend surveying your team to see what types of activities feel exciting versus tedious.

- Highlight success stories, share lessons learned, and encourage a culture of continuous learning and improvement. This is what makes it feel safe and rewarding to play. Create opportunities for team members to showcase their creative work and inspire others to think without limits.

By incorporating these principles and practices into your everyday life, you will cultivate a culture of playfulness that fosters creativity, collaboration, and innovation. Playfulness is contagious—the more you lean into it, the more those around you will feel safe to do the same. Remember, playfulness is not just a break from work—it's a powerful tool for enhancing every part of life.

Play On

Because Angelo was taught order and playfulness are mutually exclusive, and he did not grow up in an environment where it felt safe to be playful, we had to do this work slowly and over time together. To be vulnerable with me and others, he needed to have some trust that people would have his back, and would lean in and play with him. This started between us. Whenever Angelo painted a situation as all-or-nothing, black-or-white, I challenged him to at least *consider* what might live in the gray. I found myself making more jokes with Angelo, and when I'd catch him suppressing a laugh, I'd say, "Got you!" I showed up as my most playful self to show him that he could do the same. I celebrated him when he considered someone else's perspective, even for a moment. And I pointed out every example I could of how life could be disciplined and playful at the same time.

Angelo also worked on building psychological safety with his team so that he could lean into play at work. To start, he challenged himself to begin each weekly meeting with an icebreaker question. The first one was "How was your weekend?" This innocuous question felt strange to him at first because it did not directly correlate to the work at hand. But as the weeks went on, and he noticed how much his team seemed to enjoy answering, Angelo started to ask deeper questions like, "What's one item or product you can't live without?" and eventually, questions like, "Who is one person who changed your life but doesn't know it?"

Beyond the icebreakers, Angelo worked on encouraging more open-ended brainstorming in his meetings. Where before he would come in with a set agenda and plow through it systematically, he worked on posing a challenge or question to the group and giving space for people to riff on ideas, even silly or outlandish ones, without immediately shooting them down. He tried to "yes, and . . ." wherever he could. And he found that some of the most creative solutions emerged when people felt free to play with possibilities.

Angelo even started to loosen up and be more spontaneous outside of work. One weekend, some friends suggested they take an impromptu road trip to a nearby town they'd never visited. Normally, Angelo would have balked at the lack of planning. But remembering our conversations about play, he decided to go with the flow. He ended up having a wonderful, serendipitous day exploring quirky shops and sampling local cuisine. Angelo was surprised at how freeing and joyful it felt to let go of his usual rigidity.

Being more playful is a lifelong pursuit, but Angelo felt the ripples through his life pretty quickly. At work, his team dynamics improved and his reports started generating more innovative ideas. Angelo's relationships with friends and loved ones grew warmer and more accepting. He was able to roll with differences of opinion without taking everything so personally. Perhaps most important, Angelo developed a greater sense of ease and lightness in his day-to-day life. Where before he had felt constricted by his own seriousness, embracing a spirit of play opened up new avenues for fun, connection, and creativity. It was a joy to witness this transformation in Angelo, knowing the courage it took for him to step outside his comfort zone. Play, he learned, isn't frivolous or unproductive—it's an essential way of engaging with life.

PLAYING SOLO

Can play be done with a party of one? Absolutely. "Yes, and . . ." your own ideas. Practice not judging or shutting yourself down. Go to a movie, restaurant, or museum by yourself, or take a solo trip. Don't limit yourself by the social construct that certain things have to be done in a group. You don't need to go out to play, either. World-famous soccer star David Beckham literally plays for a living, and he still makes time to play on his own: After a tough practice session or game, he loves unwinding by doing LEGO projects, occasionally assembling colorful brick kits to decompress between major games. It helps him relax and alleviate the stress of the day.

Embrace spontaneity wherever you can—you're saying "yes, and . . ." to life.

The Play Push-up: Game On

Ready to play? Here's where we get to the good part. To flex your playfulness muscles, you'll have to dive into it headfirst. Here are a few games you can play one-on-one or with a larger group. They are designed to sharpen improvisational skills, establish a collaborative mindset, and unleash creative potential. Your push-up is to play one of these games (or, ideally, all three!).

YES, AND . . .

This classic improv game (similar to the restaurant ideas my friend and I riffed on) will help you get more intentional with becoming a "yes, and . . ." person. Find another person or group of people—this could be your teammates, a group of friends, your partner, or your siblings at the next family dinner—to play with you. Then, set a three-minute timer. One person will begin telling a story with a phrase or set-up. For example, someone could say "Once upon a time . . ." and then tell a line or two of the story, which can be about anything! The second person will then say, "Yes, and . . ." and add a few more lines to the story.

Here's an example:

"Once upon a time there was a lion who was launched into outer space by accident . . ."

"Yes, and the lion landed on a planet that was filled with giant gazelle . . ."

"Yes, and the lion could feel the karmic retribution the moment he set eyes on the gazelle, so he started hatching a plan . . ."

"Yes, and . . ."

Go back and forth or around the group until the three minutes are up, at which point whoever is next can conclude the story however they choose. In addition to being fun and silly, this game shows how generative brainstorming can be if people are willing to meet their partner where they are and keep it going. When I facilitate this game, I like to ask people afterward if they ever could have predicted at the beginning of the story where it would end up. They almost always laugh and say there's no way they could have seen it all coming. And this is how the most incredible ideas come to be—unexpectedly, through collaboration, and by trusting the process.

THREE THINGS IN COMMON

For this game, you'll need one partner. The two of you will have three minutes to find three unusual things that you have in common. To get there, you'll each need to ask a bunch of questions (curiosity much?): "When is your birthday?" "What is one thing you love that most people hate and one thing you hate that most people love?" "What extracurricular activities did you do in high school?"

I've played and facilitated this game countless times, and I never cease to be amazed by the things people realize they have in common. I've had two people find out that they went to the same university. I've had two people share that they both lost a parent before the age of sixteen. And I've had two people (in New York) find out that they were both from the same tiny town in Iowa (but twenty years apart). Find someone to play this with—it can be someone you've known forever (in which case you should try to find things in common you didn't know about) or someone brand new to you (this is a great game to play with new team members).

"GOT IT" / CONVERGENCE / MIND-MELD

Ready to play my favorite game of all time? I learned this one at summer camp but it's gotten popular on social media, for good reason. I've heard it called convergence or mind-meld, but I call it "Got It." This game shows how similarly we all think at a base level and makes people feel very connected in their thought processes. Although at times this game can last many rounds, it will often resolve itself quickly. For what it's worth, I have never unsuccessfully finished a round.

This game can be played with two people or one hundred people. Here's how you play. Everyone playing will try to think of a random word or common phrase. It can be anything (for example: prehistoric, banana, Thailand, Brad Pitt, hocus pocus). Whoever thinks of a unique word or common phrase first will raise their hand and say "Got it." The first two players who say "Got it" count down together, "Three, two, one," and then together say the words they were thinking of at the same time.

There are now two words in play. Next, everyone will try to think of a new word that somehow links the two words already said. There is no right way to do this—however the brain connects the words is great. So, if the first two words were *elephant* and *airplane*, your brain might connect them with the word *big*, *gray*, or *powerful*. Again, whoever thinks they have a word that connects the two initial words will say "Got it." The first two to "have it" again count down and then together say their new word. This continues on until the two people counting down say the same word at the same time (this often happens much more quickly than you would expect). There is also a way to play this game digitally—while in a video meeting, the two people who've "got it" can type their words into the chat, and then on the count of three press enter.

As with every exercise in this book, the real value of this push-up lies in the quiet reflection that follows. Ask yourself: Did you succeed in learning something unexpected? How did it feel to step outside your usual mode of interaction? Was it uncomfortable for you, for your partner or partners, for everyone? Do you feel more connected? If it was uncomfortable, did it remain so? Why do you think that might be? The more you practice this, the more agile you will get.

MY FAVORITE NONTRADITIONAL ICEBREAKER QUESTIONS

Sometimes being playful is as simple as asking a creative question. In case you ever need a go-to icebreaker that is a little outside the box, consult this list of unique questions. They range in level of intimacy—choose the one that's right for your situation.

- Who is one person who changed your life but doesn't know it?

- If you were a kitchen utensil, which one would you be and why?

- What mattered to your high school self more than anything else?

- What's one thing that you've changed your mind about lately?

- If your life is a story and at this point you're in chapter 2, when did you go from chapter 1 to chapter 2 (or in other words, what's been the most significant moment of change in your life thus far)?

- What would the title of your autobiography be?

- If you walked into a room with everyone you've ever met in it, who would you look for?

- If all of your romantic partners' personality traits / attributes were going into a bag and you could only guarantee that they'd get three of them back, which three would you choose?

- What's your hype song (the song that would play as you enter the arena)?

- F*ck, marry, kill: your own personality traits . . .

- What is something that you learned much later in life than most people?

- What's your death-row last meal (pick a main dish, two sides, a drink, and a dessert)?

- What's a story from your childhood that, looking back, predicted what you do for a living today?

- If you were on *Jeopardy!* and could pick your Final Jeopardy category, what would you pick to give yourself the best chance of winning?

- What's something that you assumed was true for everyone that you later found out is only true for you / your family?

- If you could win a lifetime supply of any one thing, what would you choose?

- What's one thing you always wanted that you have now?

- What are three words your best friend would use to describe you?

- What is one thing your parents did right? And what's one thing you wish they'd done differently?

- If you were physically invincible for one day, what would you spend the day doing?

- What is a big strength of yours that can also sometimes be a weakness?

- If you woke up tomorrow and your life had magically leveled up, how would you know? What would be different?

- The zombie apocalypse is coming—who are the three people you'd want on your team?

- What is one thing you love that most people hate, and one thing you hate that most people love?

- If you could magically develop any one skill, which would you choose?

- What is your micro superpower? (For example: can tell when it's going to rain, heightened sense of smell, can always open jars, etc.)

- Where are you, what are you doing, and who are you with when you're most content?

In his book, *Play: How It Shapes the Brain, Opens the Imagination, and Invigorates the Soul,* Dr. Stuart Brown compares play to oxygen: "Play is what lifts people out of the mundane . . . it's all around us, yet goes mostly unnoticed or unappreciated until it is missing." Just as oxygen and breathing are often unnoticed but essential factors in your physical health, playfulness is a crucial skill to strengthen for your emotional health. Prioritize it and practice it every day.

So there you have it. The seventh trait of emotional fitness. You've truly run an emotional marathon through this book. Now let's play a bit more and see how all of these traits fit together to help you continue to flex your feels and be emotionally fit.

PART III

STAYING EMOTIONALLY FIT— EVEN WHEN THINGS GET TOUGH

10
MAINTAINING AND SPREADING EMOTIONAL FITNESS

Feeling emotionally swole yet? Good! Here at the finish line, you might be feeling the burn, but I hope you're also feeling motivated, energized, and proud. The work of becoming emotionally fit is no small feat, and it's not for the faint of heart. Take a moment to recognize the accomplishment of investing in yourself—and, by extension, everyone you interact with.

Where to from here? After a real marathon, you might go out for a celebratory breakfast, or maybe just go home to soak your muscles in a hot Epsom-salt-filled bathtub. But after you replenish and recover, you don't stop running. You keep training—for the next 5K, 10K, or Ironman. The finish line of one race is the starting line of the next. Maybe you keep running just for the joy and health of it, but you know that if you stop running altogether, you'll lose the gains you've worked so hard to make. Running is about *lifelong* fitness, and emotional health is no different. Don't stop just because you've finished this book—in fact, you've really just begun.

Speaking of marathons, remember David from chapter 2? He was a superhuman in terms of physical fitness, but he faltered when it came to his emotional fitness. When his boss put him on a performance plan, he was apprehensive about his future. But David decided to dive into emotional fitness head-on. And today, I'm happy to say that he is thriving. With a ton of training on his part, and a bit of support from me, his colleagues, and his community, he created a sustained and powerful life of emotional fitness. How? He leaned into the discomfort necessary to do the work (mindfulness); he began asking for regular feedback (curiosity); he owned his part in his struggles (self-awareness); he committed himself to his performance improvement plan even when obstacles popped up (resilience); he learned to better understand the needs of his work colleagues (empathy); he learned to speak and listen more effectively (communication); and ultimately he became much more collaborative with his team (playfulness). Everyone noticed—especially his boss. He was taken off the performance plan and promoted, all within a year.

David's gains showed up in his personal life, too. When we first met, David's relationships with friends and romantic partners suffered the same precarity that his relationships at work did. Through his hard work on himself, he was able to create and maintain meaningful and rewarding relationships and gained a new sense of satisfaction with where he was in life and where he was going. In a later session, David shared that he and his partner had decided to move in together, and he was planning a trip to hike through the region of Patagonia with friends.

"I never used to even *think* about my feelings, let alone feel them," he told me. "I wasn't raised to speak the language of mental health or emotional fitness. But now that I know it, I understand everything and everyone in a completely different way."

David saw results with his emotional fitness regimen, but it took time. And he had to trust the process along the way. Unlike with physical fitness, where you can check your guns in the mirror or track your exact measurements, your journey with emotional fitness will be a little less quantitative. This is what keeps a lot of people from getting started and sticking with it. I know it's frustrating to work on something and be unsure if anything is changing. We humans have a natural inclination to quantify things: How long did I run for? How many miles did I run? How fast did I go?

But with emotional health, quality trumps quantity. Proof that you're becoming more emotionally fit might be less easily measured with numbers, but the impact will be dramatic and profound nonetheless. Keep your eyes open for the small, beautiful, and validating moments of change in your life. A conflict resolved. An interview nailed. A relationship blossomed. A fear overcome. It will show up in everything you do, slowly but surely. Life will just feel *different*.

One thing I tell my clients is that when it comes to emotional fitness, my investment is not in helping them make as much money as possible or be as successful in their business as possible (although this is what often follows as emotional fitness increases). It's to help them live as authentic and *satisfying* a life as possible. Sometimes, as people explore self-awareness and face uncomfortable truths, they realize they need a change: they should pursue a different career, move to a new city, or find a healthier relationship. As you do this work, you might have to challenge some of your assumptions about what success actually means. That's okay. Push on bravely into the life you want to live.

When David achieved his own personal best in emotional health, he didn't get a medal or shiny trophy, but he felt the weight of change—at work, at home, and in the relationships he had with himself and with everyone around him. What subtle yet powerful growth awaits you as you continue to flex your feelings? You might notice yourself feeling less reactive and overwhelmed. Life will feel less like something that happens *to* you and more like a process in which you actively participate. An argument or misunderstanding that might once have ruined your day or damaged a relationship will be an opportunity for growth and deeper connection. You might find yourself feeling less anxious, burned-out, and tired. You may feel more calm, clearheaded, and motivated. Your relationships will be healthier and more rewarding, and you will feel more satisfaction with your overall life choices.

Ultimately, all of this work is in pursuit of Aristotle's charming concept of *eudaimonia*, which roughly translates to "living well." It's a life filled with personal growth and connection that leads to a state of well-being and fulfillment. Tipping my hat to the great Greek philosopher whose theory stands the test of time, the seven traits you have read about in this book will help bring eudaimonia into your own life, just as it did for the people whose journeys you read about—from David the AI consultant, to Stephanie the marketing director, to Angelo the tech strategist. All ambitious high achievers and successful in so many ways, they struggled with their emotional fitness nonetheless. By making a commitment to show up and do the work, they now reap the benefits of a more well-rounded, emotionally fit life.

Testing, Testing

While your progress with emotional fitness isn't perfectly quantitative, you can still track your development over time. How have things shifted since you started this journey? Have you been doing your emotional push-ups? To help you gauge where you are now versus where you were when you started this book, let's return to the quiz from chapter 2.

Without looking at your original answers, retake the quiz: On a scale of 1 to 5 (with 1 meaning *This is a huge struggle for me* and 5 meaning *This is a huge strength for me*), how emotionally fit do you feel in each of the seven traits? Let's take each trait one by one.

MINDFULNESS: Do you lean into and embrace your discomfort rather than avoiding it? A mindful person is willing to be uncomfortable in order to grow.

1   2   3   4   5

CURIOSITY: Do you have a learning mindset? Can you take in tough feedback and ask tough questions? A curious person actively seeks to learn more about themself and others.

1   2   3   4   5

SELF-AWARENESS: Do you have a strong sense of self and know your triggers, biases, and emotions? A self-aware person recognizes their strengths and shortcomings.

1   2   3   4   5

RESILIENCE: Do you face life's challenges head-on and use them as an opportunity to learn and grow? A resilient person doesn't let setbacks, well, set them back (for too long).

1   2   3   4   5

EMPATHY: Do you let yourself feel the emotions and see the perspectives of others? An empathetic person can and does regularly put themself in others' shoes.

1   2   3   4   5

COMMUNICATION: Do you clearly express your needs and expectations, and listen to others in kind? A communicative person can effectively exchange ideas and thoughts.

1   2   3   4   5

PLAYFULNESS: Do you approach life with a "yes, and . . ." mindset and foster a safe space of connection and creativity? A playful person can think big and exist "in the gray."

1   2   3   4   5

Now, go back to chapter 2 and compare these answers to when you started. Have things shifted? Where did you most improve, and why might that be? Where have things stayed the same (or even regressed), and why might that be? You might have realized by reading this book that you're not as strong in one trait as you thought (if that's the case, though, give yourself more points for curiosity and self-awareness). Is there a trait that surprises you? Confuses you? Frustrates you? What else did you learn about yourself? If you feel that you are much improved, bravo. But remember, this is a lifelong endeavor. If your numbers haven't shifted much, don't give up; the most important progress in life happens slowly.

Maintaining Emotional Fitness

There is a poetic anecdote about the beauty of a lifelong pursuit: Once, a woman rushed up to the great early twentieth-century Austrian American violinist Fritz Kreisler after a performance and gushed, "I'd give my whole life to play as beautifully as you do."

Kreisler replied, "I *did*."

Emotional fitness is also a lifelong pursuit. There is no endgame. People want an easy answer for their mental health. Most mental health companies pretend to have one. But the easiest answer, truly, is to work on yourself, every single day, for the rest of your life. Accept that, and you'll be on your way. With consistent effort, you'll observe changes in your feelings, beliefs, and attitudes. Life will continue to throw you curveballs, but regular, proactive exercises will build your mental resilience to face the inevitable complexities that come your way. And like any fitness regimen, regular maintenance will also prevent more serious issues down the line. Stay limber and strong and you'll be able to face each new challenge—from an unexpected loss to an overwhelming life transition—with confidence and equanimity. Like working out your physical muscles, emotional fitness requires repetition. Here are some important ways to bolster and maintain your practice.

CHECK IN REGULARLY

Just as you get regular physicals to make sure your body is running smoothly, you should also check in on your emotional fitness periodically. Your strengths will fluctuate naturally as you go through life's challenges, and a minor struggle left unchecked can grow into a debilitating condition or issue down the line. Retake the quiz every few months to see if your numbers have shifted. It's an excellent opportunity to think about how you might adjust your emotional fitness routine.

FIND YOUR COMMUNITY

Having a community of like-minded people is a huge asset in anything you do: whether you're starting a company, starting a family, or starting a new chapter in your life, surrounding yourself with those who can understand and support you will make all the difference.

Emotional fitness is an individual journey but a communal pursuit. It's an individual journey because only you can do the work. When you go to the gym, no one can lift your weights for you. No matter how rich, smart, famous, clever, or strong you are, *you* have to lift your own weights if you want to get stronger. But it's a communal pursuit because we're all in it together. Lifting weights at the gym feels a hell of a lot more doable when you're surrounded by people who are also committed to their fitness journeys. You'll get further with a spot. Your workouts will be more effective with someone who pushes you to go a little harder, a little faster, a little longer. You can look toward the experienced bodybuilders for inspiration for where you're going, and to the newbies as a reminder of how far you've come.

The same is true with emotional fitness. No one can do this work for you. But it's going to be a lot more doable (not to mention enjoyable) when you're surrounded by like-minded people who are also committed to the work. With community supporting you, spotting you, cheering you on, and showing you new and unique ways to flex, you'll get to places you never could have gotten alone.

To find this community, put yourself out there. Talk as openly as you feel comfortable (maybe even a *little* bit uncomfortable) about the work you're doing on yourself. When you do this, you will attract others who are on the same journey and invite new people to consider getting started.

If finding new people to connect with feels like a challenge, you're definitely not alone. Research has shown that there are three conditions that facilitate the formation of new friendships in a natural way: (1) proximity (being in the same place), (2) repeated unplanned interactions, and (3) a setting that allows for letting your guard down. Ever wonder why it felt easier to make friends in high school, college, or in your early days at work than it does now? Such close and consistent settings foster friendships because you're seeing the same people over and over for a long period of time, so the relationships can form in a natural way (not to mention that complaining about cafeteria food or a frustrating boss can be quite the bonding experience).

As an adult, it's harder to make friends, especially if you work for yourself or work remotely. If that's the case, you'll need to be more intentional about it. I have a friend who is a big community builder, and he gave me this tip: reach out to two or three people you know who are working on their emotional fitness and invite them to dinner. Tell them the "cost of admission" for dinner is to bring someone that *they* know who is also interested in emotional fitness. This is a great way to meet new like-minded people and you can continue to grow your community from there. And whenever possible, connect in person—I often compare online connection to fast food—you'll get your fill and get it quickly, but it's not as long-lasting or nourishing as the real thing.

Work can also be a great place to connect to other people, especially if there's intentional space created for emotional fitness.

Former CEO of PepsiCo Indra Nooyi often encouraged her staff to connect. "We tell people to come to work and leave your [personal life] outside the door . . . except anyone who comes to work is still a mother, a father, a son, a daughter, a brother, a sister. And all the issues you have at home, you can't forget." Acknowledging that employees have lives outside work, she would often begin meetings by letting people talk about their personal lives and families. She understood that everyone comes to any relationship—whether professional or personal—as a whole person and that acknowledging that connects people on a much deeper level.

CROSS-TRAIN FOR HOLISTIC FITNESS

When it comes to physical fitness, there are no shortcuts but plenty of long-term benefits. Strengthening your core will make it more possible to work on your arms and legs, not to mention make your heart and lungs stronger and more resilient. Emotional fitness is the same. While these seven traits build on one another, they're all intertwined in so many ways. As you strengthen one, the others will naturally improve. Be sure to mix it up as you would in the gym—on any given week, you may do a run one day, lift weights on another, and hit a yoga class later in the week. This allows each muscle group to rest and recover. Flex and work out each of these emotional muscles, as they all support each other, and give yourself a break when you need it.

THE BODY FEEDS THE MIND

Although I've been comparing emotional fitness to physical fitness all through this book, I'd be remiss if I didn't specifically call out how important working on your physical health is if you want to maintain good mental and emotional health, too. How can you possibly expect yourself to be an empathetic, resilient, and playful person on four hours of sleep per night? You can't thrive in survival mode. Your body and mind are so deeply intertwined—when one is neglected, the other will be overworked to try and compensate. Just as repressing your emotions has been proven to cause a plethora of physical issues, people with poor physical health habits have significantly higher rates of anxiety, depression, and other psychological struggles. Don't underestimate the power of (even light) exercise as an antidepressant and anxiety-management tool (just thirty minutes a day can boost mood). I know the activation energy required can be tough to find (especially when you're feeling depressed or anxious), but if you can will yourself into it, it will pay off big-time.

Create Your Own Emotional Fitness Program

The pursuit of emotional fitness is a unique journey for each and every one of us. What does it look like for you? Maybe you're a strong communicator but not especially playful. Perhaps you're great at identifying your own feelings and needs but not so comfortable meeting other people in theirs. Your emotional fitness regimen should be tailored to your lifestyle, but I recommend intentionally working on each trait at least once a week. As luck would have it, there are seven traits and the week has seven days, so do one emotional push-up each day—this can be a quick and small thing (think of one thing you're grateful for) or a high-intensity exercise (have a tough conversation you've been avoiding). No matter your pace, keep at it—I promise you will see gains over time. And when it comes to integrating emotional push-ups into your everyday life, get creative! There are endless ways to apply and practice all you've learned. Here are a few push-up ideas to continue flexing each trait.

Mindfulness

- Go out in search of something that makes you a little uncomfortable and lean all the way in. Worry about rejection? Apply for a job you think you'd never be considered for in a million years, or message a celebrity on social media asking for a date.

- Dislike physical discomfort as much as I do? Take a cold plunge, or do a hot-wings challenge.

- Not a big fan of being alone? Take yourself out to dinner and a movie and sit with your incredible, whole self.

- Hooked on your phone? Practice delaying gratification and put it out of sight. Sit with your boredom and pay attention to what feelings come up.

Curiosity

- Start a compliment train: Send a message to five people in your life telling each of them what one of their big strengths is. Ask them to return the favor and then send a similar message to five people in *their* life to keep the train going. Add whatever you receive back to your self-esteem file.

- After a tough conversation, list two or three interesting new things you learned from what was said to you.

- Bust some assumptions. Write down three beliefs you have about a controversial subject. Now research reliable sources that might challenge those beliefs.

- Interview yourself. Write out ten open-ended questions you'd ask someone you find fascinating, then answer them yourself.

Self-Awareness

- Become a detective of your own mind and self. Read through old journals or look at artwork that you made as a child. Reflect on what you might have been feeling in those moments.

- Make a list of your superpowers and another list of your struggles.

- Forgive yourself for a mistake you made a long time ago.

- Ready to bring in another mind? Interview a parent, sibling, childhood teacher, or old friend. Ask them to tell you more about . . . you! Then sit with what you learn and think about how you might apply it to your current life.

Resilience

- Start a new hobby or sport like rock climbing, painting, or playing an instrument that requires persistence, growth, and learning.

- Fail on purpose. Intentionally make mistakes or suboptimal moves when playing low-stakes games, to practice losing. For example, pick weaker words on purpose in Scrabble.

- Journal about how something difficult you've been through in the past has ultimately improved your life in the present.

- Write about someone in your life (or even a fictional character) who has overcome major adversity. Study their story and mindset for inspiration.

Empathy

- Perform a random act of kindness. For example, if your workload is light, ask a loved one or teammate, "What's one thing I can take off your plate today?"

- Next time you're in a public place like a park or café, observe the people around you. Try to imagine what might be going through their minds, what their lives are like, and any challenges they could be facing.

- Read novels and short stories that explore cultures, lifestyles, and experiences different than your own. Imagine yourself stepping into the characters' shoes and seeing the world through their eyes.

- Think of a recent disagreement you've had. Write about it from the other person's point of view, or create a piece of art that reflects their motivations, feelings, and perspectives.

Communication

- In a conversation you have today (verbally or by text), find a way to share how you feel about something. For example: "I'm proud of the way we've worked together."

- Play emotional charades with friends or coworkers. Take turns acting out an emotion through expressions and body language, and have others try to guess which emotion is being conveyed.

- Do you tend to talk a lot in group settings? Commit to purposefully not speaking during your next meeting or group conversation and practice active listening instead. Do you tend to be on the quiet side? Commit to communicating one idea to the group.

- Identify jargon in your field or area of interest. Practice rephrasing those complex ideas into simple terms for different audiences. For an extra challenge, record yourself explaining these concepts and then watch it.

Playfulness

- Create a Slack channel at work and invite anyone who loves new music to join it. For the first week, think of a theme (e.g., songs of the nineties, covers better than the original, songs that make you cry in a good way), and have everyone submit one song for that theme. Then, take a vote on whose song best embodies the theme. The winner gets to pick the theme for the next week.

- Write down fun activity ideas on slips of paper, put them in a jar, and pick one out randomly whenever you need a burst of playfulness. Some ideas: "Have a picnic indoors," "Go to a museum you've never been to," or "Bake cookies and bring them to a friend."

- Explore your city like a tourist and take in the sights and sounds with fresh eyes.

- For one day, say yes to any reasonable, playful requests your friends or family make.

These are just a few ideas; with curiosity and playfulness the list is endless! And don't forget to reflect afterward on how these experiences felt. If some feel harder than others, it will give you a clue about where to focus your practice moving forward.

Spreading Emotional Fitness

One of the most powerful outcomes of working on your emotional fitness will be the ripple effect you see in the people around you. Your practice is likely to spark interest in your friends, colleagues, and loved ones who see you on the path of personal discovery. Often, the reaction they have will be quite positive. That being said, it can also feel scary or unsettling for your loved ones to see you change. When one person in a relationship changes, so will the relationship itself. Seeing others improve also puts people in touch with their own struggles. You might also find yourself feeling frustrated with *them*. When you've been working hard and have noticeably grown, you might feel impatient with people who are behind you in their development. It's the "I'm doing the work, why can't you?" phase. Stay patient and compassionate; where they are now, you once were.

People often ask me, "How can I get my husband into therapy?" or "How can I get my boss to work on her emotional fitness?" I always tell them the same thing: the best way to get other people to work on themselves is to work on yourself and be as open and transparent about your own journey as you can. I've gotten hundreds of people into therapy over the years, but it isn't by talking about my experience as a therapist. Rather, it's from talking about myself as a *client*. When I was in therapy and seeing what a big difference it made in my life, I wanted everyone in my life to do therapy, too. But it wasn't useful to tell people that they should be in therapy. So instead, I'd say, "I learned something so interesting about myself in therapy today . . . here's this epiphany I had . . . here's what's changed in my life." Inevitably, my listener's eyes would widen with interest, and eventually they would come to me and ask, "How can I try it?"

As you work on your own emotional fitness, you'll naturally start to attract more emotionally fit people into your life, and you'll be giving people permission to work on their emotional fitness. This approach is especially important if you're in a leadership position.

A hardworking founder of a B2B software company, Raj, felt like the success of the entire company rested on his efforts alone. His employees were burned-out, resentful, and disengaged—how could he possibly rely on them? So he worked nights and weekends and never took a day of vacation, even as he encouraged his employees to do a better job of maintaining their own work-life balance.

Developing his emotional fitness, Raj finally realized that the problem started with him. As soon as he started taking better care of himself, his employees felt safe to do the same. With permission to prioritize their emotional health, they started bringing their whole selves to work and the company changed course as a result.

Ultimately, developing emotional fitness improves the environment for everyone around you. Healthy emotions and behaviors are as contagious as toxic ones. By visibly investing in your own emotional fitness you give others permission to look at their own habits and tendencies. We model what people do, not what they say. Communicating with empathy makes it easier for others to reciprocate. Demonstrating playfulness encourages others to loosen up. The simple act of taking a vacation, restricting your use of email and Slack to work hours, or putting a therapy session on a shared calendar can inspire others to examine their own needs. In that sense, the most direct path to helping others will always be working on yourself. It's far better to "be the change" than to diagnose another's emotional weak spots, even if you're "right." In relationships, we often make this deal: "I'll take care of you, if you take care of me." Instead, we should say, "I'll take care of me for you, if you'll take care of you for me."

This attitude can have a ripple effect throughout your workplace and at home. I see this happen in Silicon Valley, in particular, where so much of the culture and community is rooted in the tech industry. The presence of more emotionally fit founders and leaders profoundly influences the younger generation going into the workforce, and the next generation can learn by example. If they work in an environment that teaches them to be communicative, transparent, and empathetic, they can take those lessons with them when they become the next generation of leaders and founders. You get the idea: it's a beautiful cycle of learning good emotional health that continues into the next generation.

All that said, one of the most important lessons in emotional fitness (and life) is to accept the limitations of agency you have over other people. As much as you might wish to support people in changing for the better, you *can't* actually change or control anyone but yourself. This is something most people know intellectually but have trouble accepting emotionally. When you find yourself struggling with this, try out the "let them" philosophy, introduced by author and podcaster Mel Robbins. This concept suggests that the easiest way to feel more in control of your own life is to stop trying to control other people's lives. Many people, especially those who are a little anxious or have a controlling nature (who, me?), are constantly trying to make other people feel certain things, do certain things, or avoid certain things. But in doing that, you're putting your energetic hook into someone else—and then they drag you around as you are now attached to what they do, say, and feel. So the best thing that you can do is unhook yourself, and just . . . let them. Let them do what they're going to do. Let them feel what they're going to feel. It's hugely freeing.

A Farewell Push-up

You didn't think I'd let you go without one final push-up, did you? As you reflect on how far you've come, take a moment to think about where you might go from here. One powerful exercise to solidify the changes you've begun making and the insights you've gained is to write a letter to your future self (remember, "future you" is a badass, but they still might like to hear from "present you").

In this letter, you might reflect on:

- the circumstances, challenges, hopes, or fears that led you to read this book;

- specific changes, small or large, that you have made so far on your emotional fitness journey;

- how you feel currently, both emotionally and physically;

- goals you have for your life over the next six months or year;

- encouraging words or advice you want to give to your future self.

If you're a more visual person, draw something for your future self. Whatever your approach, be honest, open, and thorough. This is a private letter just for "future you." Once finished, you have two options for sending it to your future self:

The classic paper-letter route: if you wrote the letter on paper, put it into a sealed, stamped envelope addressed to yourself. On the back, write a future date six months or a year out when you want to receive it. Then give this self-addressed letter to a trusted friend or family member and ask them to set an alarm and mail it to you on that future date.

The digital route: if you prefer to write digitally, there are free online services that allow you to schedule an email to yourself for future delivery (I like FutureMe.org). Simply compose your letter, choose your future delivery date, and their system will email it to you on that date.

Whichever method you choose, you're likely to be surprised when the letter arrives. Getting an unexpected message in your own words from "past you" can be a powerful experience—offering reassurance, inspiration, or a poignant reminder of just how far you've come.

Flex On, Fellow Feelers

For all the work you do on your emotional fitness, it's important to remember that for better or worse, life happens. There will be good days and bad. Life will treat you well, then horribly, then well again. There's an old Hebrew folk tale I love, told in various traditions, that goes something like this: An ancient king sent one of his disciples on an impossible mission. The disciple was banished from the kingdom until he could produce something that would make a sad man happy *and* a happy man sad. The disciple left the kingdom and was gone for many years, but one day, he walked back through the gates with a small stone. He brought the stone to the king and said, "I have found it—a thing that will make a sad man happy *and* a happy man sad." The king looked down at the stone placed in his hand—on it was an inscription: Gam zeh ya'avor, which translates to **This, too, shall pass**.

There will never be a life free of suffering or pain. There will rarely be even a day without challenges. But it is your reaction to those challenges that matters. And the stronger your emotional fitness, the more equipped you'll be to face all that life throws at you head-on. Flex your feelings and break an emotional sweat every day, and you'll be amazed at all that becomes possible. Will you be perfect? No, of course not. But that isn't the goal. The goal is to keep moving toward a more authentic and satisfying life, one step at a time. I want to leave you with this. Just by picking up this book, you've taken a huge step toward that life. By reading it, another step. Why stop there?

RESOURCES

Curious to read more about emotional fitness? Here is a comprehensive yet incomplete (always reading!) list of titles that have either helped me shape my own thinking or that come highly recommended by clients and colleagues.

MINDFULNESS: GETTING UNCOMFORTABLE

The Comfort Crisis: Embrace Discomfort to Reclaim Your Wild, Happy, Healthy Self by Michael Easter

Peace Is Every Step: The Path of Mindfulness in Everyday Life by Thich Nhat Hanh

The Pivot Year: 365 Days to Become the Person You Truly Want to Be by Brianna Wiest

Reach: A New Strategy to Help You Step Outside Your Comfort Zone, Rise to the Challenge, and Build Confidence by Andy Molinsky, PhD

CURIOSITY: PURSUING GROWTH

Any of Anthony Bourdain's books, really, but here are a few: *No Reservations: Around the World on an Empty Stomach; World Travel: An Irreverent Guide*; and *A Cook's Tour: Global Adventures in Extreme Cuisines*

Think Again: The Power of Knowing What You Don't Know by Adam Grant

Zen Mind, Beginner's Mind: Informal Talks on Zen Meditation and Practice by Shunryu Suzuki

SELF-AWARENESS: KNOWING THYSELF

The Artist's Way: A Spiritual Path to Higher Creativity by Julia Cameron

Burn After Writing series by Sharon Jones

The Mountain Is You: Transforming Self-Sabotage Into Self-Mastery by Brianna Wiest

RESILIENCE: BOUNCING FORWARD

Grit: The Power of Passion and Perseverance by Angela Duckworth

Man's Search for Meaning by Viktor E. Frankl

Resilient: How to Grow an Unshakable Core of Calm, Strength, and Happiness by Rick Hanson, PhD

The Upside of Shame: Therapeutic Interventions Using the Positive Aspects of a "Negative" Emotion by Vernon C. Kelly Jr. and Mary C. Lamia, PhD

EMPATHY: UNDERSTANDING OTHERS

Empathy: Why It Matters, and How to Get It by Roman Krznaric

The War for Kindness: Building Empathy in a Fractured World by Jamil Zaki

Self-Compassion: The Proven Power of Being Kind to Yourself by Kristin Neff, PhD

Leading with Empathy: Understanding the Needs of Today's Workforce by Gautham Pallapa

COMMUNICATION: SPEAKING TRUTH

Crucial Conversations: Tools for Talking When Stakes Are High by Kerry Patterson, Joseph Grenny, Ron McMillan, and Al Switzler

Nonviolent Communication: A Language of Life by Marshall B. Rosenberg, PhD

Supercommunicators: How to Unlock the Secret Language of Connection by Charles Duhigg

PLAYFULNESS: SAYING "YES, AND . . ."

Creativity, Inc.: Overcoming the Unseen Forces That Stand in the Way of True Inspiration by Ed Catmull

Yes, And: How Improvisation Reverses "No, But" Thinking and Improves Creativity and Collaboration; Lessons from the Second City by Kelly Leonard and Tom Yorton

Play: How It Shapes the Brain, Opens the Imagination, and Invigorates the Soul
by Stuart Brown, MD, with Christopher Vaughan

STAYING EMOTIONALLY FIT

Atomic Habits: An Easy and Proven Way to Build Good Habits and Break Bad Ones by James Clear

The Body Keeps the Score: Brain, Mind, and Body in the Healing of Trauma by Bessel van der Kolk, MD

Emotional Agility: Get Unstuck, Embrace Change, and Thrive in Work and Life by Susan David, PhD

No Hard Feelings: The Secret Power of Embracing Emotions at Work by Liz Fosslien and Mollie West Duffy

Radical Candor: Be a Kick-Ass Boss without Losing Your Humanity, fully revised and updated edition by Kim Scott

Burnout: The Secret to Unlocking the Stress Cycle by Emily Nagoski, PhD, and Amelia Nagoski, DMA

The Myth of Normal: Trauma, Illness, and Healing in a Toxic Culture by Gabor Maté, MD, with Daniel Maté

ACKNOWLEDGMENTS

Emotional fitness in my life has always been, first and foremost, about relationships. It would be impossible for me to adequately express my gratitude in written form for the incredible people I have in my life who have supported and loved me through my personal and professional journey, and into the best possible version of myself. To my family, friends, community, partners, colleagues, agent, editor, and publishing team—thank you for all that you do and all that you are.

NOTES

CHAPTER 2

19 **McKinsey Health Institute's 2022 survey:** McKinsey Health Institute, "Addressing Employee Burnout: Are You Solving the Right Problem?," May 27, 2022, https://www.mckinsey.com/mhi/our-insights/addressing -employee-burnout-are-you-solving-the-right-problem.

19 **National Center for Health Statistics reported:** National Center for Health Statistics, "Anxiety and Depression: Household Pulse Survey, 2020–2024," last reviewed August 21, 2024, https://www.cdc.gov/nchs /covid19/pulse/mental-health.htm.

19 **All this can lead to more stress and burnout:** Amy Novotney, "Why Mental Health Needs to Be a Top Priority in the Workplace," American Psychological Association, October 21, 2022, updated April 21, 2023, https://www.apa.org/news/apa/2022/surgeon-general-workplace-well -being.

20 **compared to 40 percent:** "Black Mental Health: What You Need to Know," McLean Hospital, July 15, 2024, https://www.mcleanhospital .org/essential/black-mental-health.

CHAPTER 3

47 **On a 2022 episode of the podcast:** Lorne Michaels, "Lorne Michaels (Part 1)," interview by Dana Carvey and David Spade, *Fly on the Wall*, October 7, 2022, 48:20, https://youtu.be/5ny8Xf9OoRA.

49 **a threat into an opportunity:** Alison Wood Brooks, "Get Excited: Reap-praising Pre-Performance Anxiety as Excitement," *Journal of Experimental*

Psychology: General 143, no. 3 (2014): 1144–58, https://doi.org /10.1037/a0035325.

CHAPTER 4

83 **According to researchers at Harvard:** K. Huang et al., "It Doesn't Hurt to Ask: Question-asking Increases Liking," *Journal of Personality and Social Psychology* 113, no. 3 (September 2017): 430–52, https://www.hbs .edu/faculty/Pages/item.aspx?num=52115.

CHAPTER 5

95 **While most people *believe* they are self-aware:** Tasha Eurich, "What Self-Awareness Really Is (and How to Cultivate It)," *Harvard Business Review*, January 4, 2018, https://hbr.org/2018/01/what-self-awareness -really-is-and-how-to-cultivate-it.

99 **When you're self-aware, you will make better decisions:** Katherine Kam, "Self-Awareness Can Improve Relationships. Here Are Tips to Build It," *The Washington Post*, November 26, 2022, https://www.wash ingtonpost.com/wellness/2022/11/26/self-awareness-emotional -intelligence/.

99 **better manage your emotions:** Manuel London, Valerie I. Sessa, and Loren A. Shelley, "Developing Self-Awareness: Learning Processes for Self- and Interpersonal Growth," *Annual Review of Organizational Psychology and Organizational Behavior* 10 (January 2023): 261–88, https:// doi.org/10.1146/annurev-orgpsych-120920-044531.

99 **You will be a more confident:** Paul J. Silvia and Maureen E. O'Brien, "Self-Awareness and Constructive Functioning: Revisiting 'the Human Dilemma,'" *Journal of Social and Clinical Psychology* 23, no. 4 (August 2004): 475–89, https://doi.org/10.1521/jscp.23.4.475.40307.

99 **show up better for your colleagues and coworkers:** Anna Sutton, Helen M. Williams, and Christopher W. Allinson, "A Longitudinal, Mixed Method Evaluation of Self-Awareness Training in the Work-place," *European Journal of Training and Development* 39, no. 7 (August 2015): 610–27, https://doi.org/10.1108/EJTD-04-2015-0031.

103 **rather than sit and think:** Timothy D. Wilson et al., "Just Think: The Challenges of the Disengaged Mind," *Science* 345, no. 6192 (July 2014): 75–77, https://doi.org/10.1126/science.1250830.

CHAPTER 6

129 according to the experts: Amanda Reill, "A Simple Way to Make Better Decisions," *Harvard Business Review*, December 5, 2023, https://hbr.org /2023/12/a-simple-way-to-make-better-decisions.

132 According to the US Census Bureau Household Pulse Survey: KFF, "Latest Federal Data Show That Young People Are More Likely Than Older Adults to Be Experiencing Symptoms of Anxiety or Depression," news release, March 20, 2023, https://www.kff.org/mental-health /press-release/latest-federal-data-show-that-young-people-are-more -likely-than-older-adults-to-be-experiencing-symptoms-of-anxiety-or -depression/.

133 Too little anxiety: "Yerkes–Dodson Law," *Oxford Reference*, accessed September 9, 2024, https://www.oxfordreference.com/display/10.1093 /oi/authority.20110803125332105.

CHAPTER 7

148 "psychological 'superglue' that connects people": K. N. C., "How to Increase Empathy and Unite Society," *The Economist*, June 7, 2019, https://www.economist.com/open-future/2019/06/07/how-to-increase -empathy-and-unite-society.

148 increases understanding, trust, and connection: Elizabeth A. Segal, "Five Ways Empathy Is Good for Your Health," *Psychology Today*, December 17, 2018, https://www.psychologytoday.com/us/blog/social -empathy/201812/five-ways-empathy-is-good-your-health.

148 the overall satisfaction of a relationship: Mark H. Davis and H. Alan Oathout, "Maintenance of Satisfaction in Romantic Relationships: Empathy and Relational Competence," *Journal of Personality and Social Psychology* 53, no. 2 (1987): 397–410, https://doi.org/10.1037/0022-3514.53 .2.397.

149 In one study, researchers assigned: Linda H. Jütten, Ruth E. Mark, and Margriet M. Sitskoorn, "Empathy in Informal Dementia Caregivers and Its Relationship with Depression, Anxiety, and Burden," *International Journal of Clinical and Health Psychology* 19, no. 1 (January 2019): 12–21, https://doi.org/10.1016/j.ijchp.2018.07.004.

149 lower stress and anxiety levels: Jamil Zaki, "It's Cool to Be Kind: The Value of Empathy at Work," interview by Bryan Hancock and Brooke

Weddle, *McKinsey Talks Talent*, podcast, February 28, 2024, 34:21, https://www.mckinsey.com/capabilities/people-and-organizational-performance/our-insights/its-cool-to-be-kind-the-value-of-empathy-at-work.

149 **build trust and collaboration:** Francis X. Frei and Anne Morriss, "Begin with Trust," *Harvard Business Review*, May–June 2020, https://hbr.org/2020/05/begin-with-trust.

149 **by an empathetic boss:** Tracy Brower, "Empathy Is the Most Important Leadership Skill according to Research," *Forbes*, September 19, 2021, updated January 12, 2022, https://www.forbes.com/sites/tracybrower/2021/09/19/empathy-is-the-most-important-leadership-skill-according-to-research/.

149 **Empathy also fosters more empathy:** Arunas L. Radzvilavicius, Alexander J. Stewart, and Joshua B. Plotkin, "Evolution of Empathetic Moral Evaluation," ed. *eLife* 8 (April 2019): e44269, https://doi.org/10.7554/eLife.44269.

149 **less empathetic leaders:** Brower, "Empathy."

151 **picked up from family and environment:** University of Cambridge, "Genes Play a Role in Empathy," *ScienceDaily*, March 12, 2018, https://www.sciencedaily.com/releases/2018/03/180312085124.htm.

151 **more naturally occurring oxytocin:** A. M. Barchi-Ferreira and F. L. Osório, "Associations between Oxytocin and Empathy in Humans: A Systematic Literature Review," *Psychoneuroendocrinology* 129 (July 2021): 105268, https://doi.org/10.1016/j.psyneuen.2021.105268.

151 **men to be less emotional:** Leonardo Christov-Moore et al., "Empathy: Gender Effects in Brain and Behavior," *Neuroscience & Biobehavioral Reviews* 46, no. 4 (October 2014): 604–27, https://doi.org/10.1016/j.neubiorev.2014.09.001.

153 **which is critical to empathy:** William W. Maddux, Hajo Adam, and Adam D. Galinsky, "When in Rome . . . Learn Why the Romans Do What They Do: How Multicultural Learning Experiences Facilitate Creativity," *Personality and Social Psychology Bulletin* 36, no. 6 (June 2010): 731–41, https://doi.org/10.1177/0146167210367786; Brent Crane, "For a More Creative Brain, Travel," *The Atlantic*, March 31, 2015, https://www.theatlantic.com/health/archive/2015/03/for-a-more-creative-brain-travel/388135/.

156 **"acute inability to empathize":** Adam Waytz, "The Limits of Empathy,"

Harvard Business Review, January 1, 2016, https://hbr.org/2016/01/the -limits-of-empathy.

156 **can dampen hope:** Debbie L. Stoewen, "Moving from Compassion Fatigue to Compassion Resilience Part 4: Signs and Consequences of Compassion Fatigue," *The Canadian Veterinary Journal* 61, no. 11 (November 2020): 1207–9, https://www.ncbi.nlm.nih.gov/pmc/articles /PMC7560777/.

159 **In fact, research shows that:** J. Austin, C. H. C. Drossaert, and E. T. Bohlmeijer, "Self-Compassion as a Resource of Resilience," in *Handbook of Self-Compassion,* ed. Amy Finlay-Jones, Karen Bluth, and Kristin Neff, Mindfulness in Behavioral Health (Cham, Switzerland: Springer Nature, 2023), 165–82, https://doi.org/10.1007/978-3-031-22348-8_10.

161 **empathize better with things we understand:** Jacob Israelashvili, Disa A. Sauter, and Agneta H. Fischer, "Different Faces of Empathy: Feelings of Similarity Disrupt Recognition of Negative Emotions," *Journal of Experimental Social Psychology* 87 (March 2020): 103912, https:// doi.org/10.1016/j.jesp.2019.103912.

CHAPTER 8

167 **twenty hours per week:** Leeron Hoory and Kelly Main, "The State of Workplace Communication in 2024," *Forbes Advisor,* March 8, 2023, https://www.forbes.com/advisor/business/digital-communication -workplace/.

173 **profound impact of nonverbal behavior:** Nalini Ambady and Robert Rosenthal, "Half a Minute: Predicting Teacher Evaluations from Thin Slices of Nonverbal Behavior and Physical Attractiveness," *Journal of Personality and Social Psychology* 64, no. 3 (March 1993): 431–41, https:// doi.org/10.1037/0022-3514.64.3.431.

179 **by psychologist Marshall Rosenberg:** Mark Abadi, "When CEO Satya Nadella Took Over Microsoft, He Started Defusing Its Toxic Culture by Handing Each of His Execs a 15-Year-Old Book by a Psychologist," *Business Insider,* October 7, 2018, https://www.businessinsider.com /microsoft-satya-nadella-nonviolent-communication-2018-10.

CHAPTER 9

197 **"Play functions to sustain":** M. Parsons, "The Logic of Play in Psycho-analysis," *The International Journal of Psycho-Analysis* 80, no. 5 (October 1999): 871–84, https://pubmed.ncbi.nlm.nih.gov/10643568.

197 **"Karate training is not a real fight":** Parsons, "Logic of Play."

198 **boost creativity (and therefore productivity):** Samuel West, "Playing at Work: Organizational Play as a Facilitator of Creativity," PhD diss., Department of Psychology, Lund University, 2015.

198 **deepen community (fewer office politics):** "Playing Up the Benefits of Play at Work," Association for Psychological Science, October 13, 2017, https://www.psychologicalscience.org/news/minds-business/playing-up-the-benefits-of-play-at-work.html.

198 **worked to create fresh storylines:** Nicole LaPorte, "How Shondaland Built a Creative Work Culture with Play-Doh, Treadmills, and Bake-offs," *Fast Company*, August 8, 2017, https://www.fastcompany.com/40438335/how-shondaland-built-a-creative-work-culture-with-play-doh-treadmills-and-bakeoffs.

199 **enabled survival into adulthood:** Jennifer Wallace, "Why It's Good for Grown-Ups to Go Play," *The Washington Post*, May 20, 2017, https://www.washingtonpost.com/national/health-science/why-its-good-for-grown-ups-to-go-play/2017/05/19/99810292-fd1f-11e6-8ebe-6e0dbe4f2bca_story.html.

199 **In their seminal work on play theory:** Peter K. Smith and Jaipaul L. Roopnarine, eds., "Editorial Introduction," in *The Cambridge Handbook of Play: Developmental and Disciplinary Perspectives* (Cambridge, UK: Cambridge University Press, 2018), i–ii.

200 **need for stable relationships:** Michael Yogman et al., Committee on Psychosocial Aspects of Child and Family Health, Council on Communications and Media,et al., "The Power of Play: A Pediatric Role in Enhancing Development in Young Children," *Pediatrics* 142, no. 3 (September 2018): e20182058, https://doi.org/10.1542/peds.2018-2058.

200 **their own innate curiosity:** Nick Morrison, "Children Learn More through Play Than from Teacher-Led Instruction," *Forbes*, January 12, 2022, https://www.forbes.com/sites/nickmorrison/2022/01/12/children-learn-more-through-play-than-from-teacher-led-instruction/.

200 **a sense of independence and confidence:** "Learning through Play," Unicef, October 2018, https://www.unicef.org/sites/default/files/2018 -12/UNICEF-Lego-Foundation-Learning-through-Play.pdf.

200 **"It is only in playing":** D. W. Winnicott, *Playing and Reality*, 2nd ed., Routledge Classics (Hoboken: Taylor and Francis, 2012).

200 **criminal activities and violence as adults:** Stuart Brown, "Play Deprivation Can Damage Early Child Development," *Child and Family Blog* (blog), October 2018, https://childandfamilyblog.com/play-deprivation -early-child-development/.

200 **"The opposite of play":** Brian Sutton-Smith, *The Ambiguity of Play* (Cambridge, MA: Harvard University Press, 2001).

200 **calming nerves and diffusing stress:** Cale D. Magnuson and Lynn A. Barnett, "The Playful Advantage: How Playfulness Enhances Coping with Stress," *Leisure Sciences* 35, no. 2 (March 2013): 129–44, https://doi .org/10.1080/01490400.2013.761905.

200 **indulge in too much screen time:** Christopher Townsend et al., "The Effectiveness of Gaming Interventions for Depression and Anxiety in Young People: Systematic Review and Meta-Analysis," *BJPsych Open* 8, no. 1 (January 2022): e25, https://doi.org/10.1192/bjo.2021.1078.

201 **happier and more creative:** Tamlin S. Conner, Colin G. DeYoung, and Paul J. Silvia, "Everyday Creative Activity as a Path to Flourishing," *The Journal of Positive Psychology* 13, no. 2 (March 4, 2018): 181–89, https://doi .org/10.1080/17439760.2016.1257049.

201 **clock keep ticking for longer:** Kaori Sakurada et al., "Associations of Frequency of Laughter with Risk of All-Cause Mortality and Cardiovascular Disease Incidence in a General Population: Findings from the Yamagata Study," *Journal of Epidemiology* 30, no. 4 (April 2020): 188–93, https://doi.org/10.2188/jea.JE20180249.

201 **can add on eight years to your life:** Solfrid Romundstad et al., "A 15-Year Follow-Up Study of Sense of Humor and Causes of Mortality: The Nord-Trøndelag Health Study," *Psychosomatic Medicine* 78, no. 3 (April 2016): 345–53, https://doi.org/10.1097/PSY.0000000000000275.

203 **known as Project Aristotle:** Charles Duhigg, "What Google Learned from Its Quest to Build the Perfect Team," *The New York Times Magazine*, February 25, 2016, https://www.nytimes.com/2016/02/28/maga zine/what-google-learned-from-its-quest-to-build-the-perfect-team .html.

215 **unwinding by doing LEGO projects:** Amanda Goh, "David Beckham Is a Lego Geek and Says the Toys Help to Calm Him Down," *Business Insider*, October 8, 2023, https://www.businessinsider.com/david -beckham-loves-lego-helps-to-calm-him-down-2023-10.

215 **decompress before major games:** Wallace, "Why It's Good."

CHAPTER 10

233 **Research has shown:** Alex Williams, "Why Is It Hard to Make Friends Over 30?" *The New York Times*, July 13, 2012, https://www.nytimes.com /2012/07/15/fashion/the-challenge-of-making-friends-as-an-adult .html.

234 **"We tell people to come":** Jane Hanson, "PepsiCo's Indra Nooyi, the Queen of Pop, Shares Her Tips for Bringing Compassionate Leadership to Work," *Forbes*, April 30, 2022, https://www.forbes.com/sites/janehan son/2022/04/30/pepsicos-indra-nooyi-the-queen-of-pop-shares-her -tips-for-bringing-compassionate-leadership-to-work/.

235 **a plethora of physical issues:** Peter Economy, "9 Really Bad Things That Happen to Your Health When You Avoid Feeling Your Emotions," *Inc.*, April 28, 2019, https://www.inc.com/peter-economy/9-really-bad-things -that-happen-to-your-health-when-you-avoid-feeling-your-emotions .html.

235 **and other psychological struggles:** Felipe Barreto Schuch and Davy Vancampfort, "Physical Activity, Exercise, and Mental Disorders: It Is Time to Move On," *Trends in Psychiatry and Psychotherapy* 43, no. 3 (October 2021): 177–84, https://doi.org/10.47626/2237-6089-2021 -0237.

235 **just thirty minutes a day can boost mood:** "Caring for Your Mental Health," National Institute of Mental Health (NIMH), February 2024, https://www.nimh.nih.gov/health/topics/caring-for-your-mental -health.

242 **the next generation of leaders and founders:** "Hit the Emotional Gym—The Founder's Framework for Emotional Fitness," First Round Review, May 26, 2020, https://review.firstround.com/hit-the-emotional -gym-the-founders-framework-for-emotional-fitness/.

INDEX

INDEX

boundaries
    benefits of, 157
    boundaried vulnerability, 190–92
    client-therapist, 156–57
    and empathy, 156, 171
    setting, 157–58, 171
    taking on too much, 155–56
Bourdain, Anthony, 82–83, 153
the brain's resistance to change, 39
Brown, Stuart, 200, 221
burnout
    preventing, 135–37
    in the workplace, 8, 18–19

C
Caitlyn case study (feeling stuck), 125–27,
    134–35
Camilla case study (intuition), 54–55
Cara case study (self-awareness), 116–17
case studies
    Angelo (playfulness), 195–96, 204,
        205–06, 213–14
    Ari (resilience), 119–23, 127, 131–32
    Benjamin (self-awareness), 106
    Caitlyn (feeling stuck), 125–27, 134–35
    Camilla (intuition), 54–55
    Cara (self-awareness), 116–17
    Corey (fear of success), 138–39
    David (becoming an emotionally fit
        person), 13–15, 226–27
    Emma (asking questions), 85–86
    Fenty Beauty, 150
    Jamie (avoiding confrontation), 52–53
    Keller (self-awareness), 101–02
    Lana (curiosity), 80–82
    Meghan (mindfulness), 35–38, 39–40,
        56–58, 172
    Monica (workplace difficulties), 6–7
    OXO kitchen utensils, 150
    Patagonia, 150
    Raj (developing emotional fitness), 241
    Robin (fear of making a career
        change), 50–51

Stephanie (communication), 165–66,
    173–74, 178, 181–82, 183–84, 192
Steven (curiosity), 63–67, 78–80
Valerie (self-awareness), 91–95, 96,
    111–12
Will (empathy), 145–48, 153–55, 158–59
challenges
    adaptability, 124–25
    of life, 244–45
    as a springboard for growth, 123
change
    the brain's resistance to, 39
    making gradual changes, 51
    reflecting on your experiences, 51
    the ripple effects of developing
        emotional fitness, 240–42
    willingness to, 22–23
childhood
    the role of play in, 205–06
    self-reflecting on the defenses
        developed during, 80
choices, making
    agency, 28, 242
    author's experiences, 128–29
    life as a series of, 129
    sunk-cost fallacy, 130–31
Chouinard, Yvon, 150
Clear, James, 48
closure and closure ceremonies, 127–28, 130
Coa, 12, 114, 164, 188
coaching from a trained therapist, 107–11
communication
    body language, 173
    boundaried vulnerability, 190–92
    complaining without blaming, 185–86
    conflict, 173–76
    and curiosity, 170
    defined, 167
    and discomfort, 169
    emojis, 188–90
    and empathy, 170–71
    importance of, 24
    listening, 84–85, 87, 171–72

262

ABOUT THE AUTHOR

Dr. Emily Anhalt studied psychology at the University of Michigan and earned her master's and doctorate degrees in clinical psychology at the Wright Institute in Berkeley, California. Dr. Anhalt has consulted with some of the fastest-growing technology companies in the world, such as Google, Asana, Spotify, NBCUniversal, and TEDx. In 2019, she cofounded the mental health start-up Coa, the gym for mental health, and consulted for American Express and the NBA, among other companies. Her writing has been featured in *The New York Times*, *The Wall Street Journal*, *Harvard Business Review*, and *Wired*. She currently splits her time between San Francisco and New York City.